A Nail, A R

Madeleine Bourdouxhe was born in 1906 in Liège. Her novels include *La Femme de Gilles*, published by Gallimard in 1937, recently reissued in Belgium and France and shortly to be published for the first time in English by Lime Tree, and *A la recherche de Marie* (Brussels, 1943), also recently reissued in France. In the war, she refused to be published by firms that had been taken over by the Germans, and until recently her work has appeared mainly in literary magazines. She is an active member of the Libre Académie de Belgique, an organisation devoted to encouraging the work of Belgian writers and artists. She lives in Brussels and has one daughter, Marie.

Faith Evans is an editor, agent and critic. Her publications include Rebecca West's *Family Memories*, which she introduced and edited, and *The Daughters of Karl Marx: Family Correspondence 1866–98*, which she translated and edited. She is a founder member of the Women in Publishing group.

Madeleine Bourdouxhe

A Nail, A Rose

and other stories

Translated and introduced
by Faith Evans

LIME
TREE

First published in Great Britain 1989
by The Women's Press
This edition published 1992
by Lime Tree
an imprint of the Octopus Publishing Group
Michelin House, 81 Fulham Rd, London SW3 6RB
and distributed in the United States of America by
HEB Inc., 361 Hanover Street, Portsmouth, New Hampshire 03801

Sept Nouvelles first published 1985 by Editions Tierce, Paris

Sous le pont Mirabeau first published 1944 by Editions Libris, Brussels

Translation and introduction copyright © Faith Evans, 1989
Copyright of *Sept Nouvelles* © Editions Tierce, 1985
Copyright of *Sous le pont Mirabeau* by Madeleine Bourdouxhe, 1944

This translation has been made possible
in part through a grant from
the Wheatland Foundation.

The author and translator have
asserted their moral rights.

A CIP catalogue record for this book
is available from the British Library
ISBN 0 413 45491 6

Printed in Great Britain
by Cox & Wyman Ltd, Reading

Contents

Introduction

It is over half a century since Madeleine Bourdouxhe made her name in Paris with her novel *La Femme de Gilles*. Four decades have passed since Simone de Beauvoir praised her in *The Second Sex*. Yet, astonishingly, this is the first volume of her work ever to appear in English. There has been a long period of neglect: even in Belgium, her native country, and in France, where many of her stories were originally published, she is only now being discovered by feminist critics.[1]

When I first read her work in French in 1987 I recognised a confident feminist vision that, though born of time and place, still spoke with an exciting directness. I was drawn to the author's quiet strength. As I began to translate her stories and to engage with the subtle rhythms of her prose, my curiosity developed into commitment, so that I felt impelled to discover more about her life, and the social and cultural context from which she had come. Unearthing this information, however, was more problematic; not only is little of her work in print, but she has gone almost unnoticed by literary historians. The only solution was to seek her out for myself.

By the time I visited Madeleine Bourdouxhe in her Brussels apartment in July 1988 I had finished translating the stories, read most of her other work in libraries, and made many guesses, some of which turned out to be more inspired than others. I had thought of her as a wartime author, had assumed, because of the difficulty in tracking down her work, that her writing career was long over, so the biggest and most welcome surprise was that she had continued to write: indeed, three of the stories in *A Nail, A*

1 See Bibliographical Note.

Rose ('Clara', 'Blanche' and 'René') are quite recent. Even now, she still works through the night; a young friend of hers told me that she has often seen the lights on in her apartment when returning home late from a concert in the Grande Place, until recently her *quartier*.

An elegant, straightforward woman in her early eighties, naturally reticent, though clearly delighted at the idea of having her work translated ('The English were the first to liberate Brussels'), Madeleine Bourdouxhe told me enough about herself to justify my considering her work in the light of her life. As she talked, I began to see that the long neglect is partly explained by her diffidence but even more by the catastrophic disruptions of modern European history. From the start, I realised, hers has been a career shaped by the need for resistance, in all its forms.

Madeleine Bourdouxhe was born in Liège in 1906. After a short period in Paris as a child, the family returned to Belgium at the end of the First World War, later moving to Brussels, where Madeleine studied at a lycée and then read philosophy at the university. In 1927 she married a mathematician, Jacques Muller, and gave private lessons in French, Latin and history.

The people she chose to recall at our meeting gave me an important clue to her politics. In the thirties, she told me, one of her closest friends, whose work she passionately admired, was the Russian revolutionary writer Victor Serge. Serge was foremost among the intellectuals who saw through Stalin and spoke against the frame-up of the Moscow trials. Deported to Siberia in 1933 for his association with Trotsky, he was expelled from the Soviet Union after protests organised by André Gide, and he and his son found refuge with Madeleine Bourdouxhe and her husband in Brussels, his native town – 'Someone brought him to me,' she said. He moved to Paris before the war and she would often visit him to talk about politics, life and work: 'We were politically of one mind, both of us much preoccupied with the Spanish Civil War.' Serge's commitment to *lucidité* and *probité* (political honesty) is indeed similar to that of Madeleine Bourdouxhe as revealed in her stories. In his *Notebooks* he defines the impetus to write as 'a means of living several destinies, of penetration into others, of communicating with them. The writer becomes conscious of the world he brings to life, he is its consciousness and he thus escapes from the ordinary limits of the self, something which is at once intoxicating and enriching.'[2]

By the middle of the 1930s Madeleine Bourdouxhe had produced several novels and stories. 'I've always had a passion for writing,' she told me. 'Even as a child I wrote little descriptions of landscape or made up stories.' Visiting Paris to submit her work to publishers, she was taken up by Jean Paulhan, editor of the *Nouvelle Revue Française* and reader for the house of Gallimard. Paulhan had a reputation for seeking out new writers and encouraging them to express their convictions in their work; his other finds included Marcel Aymé and Raymond Queneau. On Paulhan's recommendation *La Femme de Gilles* was accepted by Gallimard and was published, to great acclaim, in 1937. The literary critic and novelist Ramon Fernandez wrote, 'The art of conveying silence – the most difficult of all the novelist's tasks – is here flawlessly achieved.'

Then came the Second World War, the trigger for the short stories Madeleine Bourdouxhe was to produce over the next decade, five of which are included in *A Nail, A Rose*. As she talked to me in 1988 I began to see why the Occupation overshadows so many of her stories and her consciousness of herself, and to have some perception of what it means when your country is overtaken by a foreign power, especially when you yourself are patriotic but not in the least nationalistic. It's no wonder that as a writer she has always been so preoccupied with borders and frontiers, with people who take risks, people whose lives have to be lived underground. She has experienced displacement for herself.

Madeleine Bourdouxhe's own war experiences are most dramatically reflected in *Sous le pont Mirabeau*, the final long story in this volume, a moving, outspoken celebration of maternity seen in the light of the destructive futility of war. The novella appears here for the first time since its original publication in 1944.

---

2 *Carnets*, Paris, 1952. For a useful biographical sketch of Serge see Richard Greeman's introduction to the most recent edition of *Midnight in the Century*, Writers & Readers, London, 1982.

Sous le pont Mirabeau takes place in May 1940, the month of the German invasion of Belgium, less than a year after the war began. A week later the French army in the Meuse was on the retreat and the Germans were ranging over the French countryside. After the capitulation of the French and the establishment of the collaborationist Pétain government in Vichy, both countries became a morass of displaced persons trying to escape the Occupation.

Madeleine Bourdouxhe was among them. On the day of the invasion she had just given birth to her first child, Marie, in a Brussels maternity home and, helped by family and friends, made her precarious way through France to a village near Bordeaux.

Obliged to return home to Brussels later that year under orders from the exiled Belgian government, she remained there for the rest of the war. Her publishing activities were now severely curtailed by circumstance. Not only was she politically suspect, but along with her editor Jean Paulhan she refused to set foot in, never mind be published by, publishing houses such as Gallimard and Grasset that had been taken over by the Germans. She was anxious to help with Resistance work, and hid escaping Jewish women refugees in her house in Brussels. She found it difficult to get a permit to visit occupied Paris, and when she did, it was at great danger to her life. Once, she now says with a laugh, she persuaded 'a decent Nazi' to issue her with a permit by bribing him with a signed copy of *La Femme de Gilles*.

Whilst researching Madeleine Bourdouxhe's background I had speculated on the possible influence of Paul Eluard, the most sensitive and aware of the male Surrealists, whose poetic imagery, in poems like 'La Vie immédiate' (1932), had seemed to me sometimes to prefigure her own. This made doubly intriguing her reference to Eluard as her Resistance 'contact' in the war: she had, she told me, collected anit-Nazi leaflets from his Paris apartment to take back to Belgium. But any suggestion of a literary connection brought forth a polite but vehement denial: no one had had any effect upon her work. However, even artists working in comparative isolation cannot be immune to the intellectual currents around them, and Madeleine Bour-douxhe, essentially a political writer, very likely absorbed – consciously or unconsciously – just as much as was necessary in order to express her own individual voice.

Most of the stories in *A Nail, A Rose* were written in the aftermath not only of Nazi tyranny but of pre-war Surrealism. Ever since its 1924 manifesto the Surrealist movement had been calling for an art that would reconcile dream and reality, the interior and the exterior world, while for the most part putting forward such wildly idealistic political programmes as reconciling Marx and Freud. Though disrupted by the war, the movement continued to flourish in America. But in Europe, the experience of having been occupied, further revelations of Nazi atrocities and a growing awareness of Stalinist oppression encouraged writers to turn to versions of existentialism, with its emphasis on individual choice and its appeal to the artist's personal sense of responsibility. It was a period, then, when the options for European writers were as diverse as they had ever been, when their ideological functions were continually subject to scrutiny and debate.

Paul Eluard and his wife Nusch were among the few members of the Surrealist movement to remain in Paris during the Occupation, many of the others having fled to New York and Mexico, to the annoyance of Jean-Paul Sartre who, in 1945, proclaimed that the social and political responsibility of the writer was to 'engage with his period', to 'guide the reader, expose injustice and provoke indignation'.[3]

This was the principle upon which he, Simone de Beauvoir, Raymond Aron and others founded *Les Temps Modernes*, and Madeleine Bourdouxhe was clearly a writer whose viewpoint, if not her writing style, accorded with the prescription. By comparison with some of the other French literary journals of the time, *Les Temps Modernes* was also enlightened in its attitude to women. At the end of the war Sartre and de Beauvoir would meet Madeleine Bourdouxhe in Paris cafés on her trips from Brussels – and 'Les Jours de la femme Louise' appeared in the journal in January 1947.

In the same issue there was an article by Nathalie Sarraute on Paul Valéry, an extract from Richard Wright's *Jeunesse Noire* (*Black Boy*) and an article by Simone de Beauvoir entitled 'Pour une morale de l'ambiguité'. Reading the magazine forty years

3 *Les Temps Modernes*, February–June 1947.

later, what is striking is the modernity of Madeleine Bourdouxhe's style, her lack of dogmatism and the poetic simplicity of her manner: traits that have remained remarkably consistent over the years. But most of all, her writing stands out from the rest for its concern with the inner world of women.

Translated here as 'Louise', the story is one of the few in *A Nail, A Rose* to contain a middle-class character; and even then 'Madame' is really only there as a catalyst for understanding her maid Louise. 'Louise' shows the ideal of female empathy cut across by the absolute barrier of class. Louise dreams of friendship with Madame; men keep her hanging around but Madame, elegant and mysterious, never lets her down; indeed, on Louise's night off she lends her a smart blue coat. Louise wanders around the Paris night in a state of delirium; in a café, her pen dictates a 'cabalistic message of love' (possibly a teasing reference to the 'automatic writing' of the Surrealists). But can Louise ever really inhabit the blue coat? One recalls Jean Genet's reply to the bourgeois lady who told him that her maid ought to be very happy, since she gave her all her old dresses. 'Excellent,' replied Genet. 'And does she give you hers?'

Madeleine Bourdouxhe draws the characters for her stories not from fashionable Parisian society but from the suburbs and the provinces, from the old vegetable market in Les Halles, from unremarkable factory towns in Lorraine or the Meuse. The milieux she has always chosen to describe are essentially working-class. She prefers to observe the margins from the margins and form her own view of society: as she proudly told me, 'I write what I see.'

Yet she is not in any simple sense a realist. Setting her work in proletarian environments enables her to cut right through to the full range of women's responsibilities, and to reach out to a confident purity of style. Her method of achieving this purity is the world of the dream. In all her stories she draws upon the dream to pursue her own very personal quest for the nature of female identity and the liberation of the female spirit.

It is the world of the dream that suggests a historical link between Madeleine Bourdouxhe, whose work is essentially painterly and poetic, and the women artists associated with the Surrealist movement. Like them, she was sympathetic to the spirit of revolt and to experimentation, forming part of no clique or coterie, and fiercely resistant to organised activity. This was probably wise, since from Apollinaire on, events have shown that women involved with Surrealism are especially susceptible to the risk that naming, as child or as muse, might mean being claimed too. The process of being idealised carries its own dangers, gives women a statutory place, at once adored and unrecognised, in the false order of a male-defined culture. All in all, it's safer to possess a vision of your own.

The women artists working in the 1940s eliminated the barriers between the conscious and the sub-conscious, the rational and the irrational, life and art; and they set as high a value upon the dream as the male Surrealists. But by stressing women's biological and spiritual resources, 'mysteries' that were both female and active, they could claim a special relationship with creative nature and the cosmos that endowed them with a special, superior wisdom.[4]

Madeleine Bourdouxhe sometimes uses this surreal symbolism for her own feminist ends too, if more discreetly and less fantastically than her artistic contemporaries. She relies upon images that distort and disturb, that belong to nightmare: monstrous insects with glossy black shells, a chignon surprisingly held in place with nails instead of hairpins.

She is intrigued, too, by the relationship between personal memory and the passage of time as they affect the female sensibility. Many of her most ambitious stylistic experiments involve this exploration. In several of the stories women abandon themselves unrestrainedly to remembered time until, in an organic layering of memory upon memory upon memory, the present seems to explode in a marvellous fusion of related images. Sensuously delving into your unconscious will lead you to an intense and heightened sense of yourself which will sustain you in moments of extremity – when a man leaves you or beats you up, or when you are alone in the intolerable heat of a summer night, on an army lorry with blood dripping down your legs, unable to satisfy your newborn infant's unbearable demands. The capacity to connect experience and memory, she

4 See Whitney Chadwick, *Women Painters and the Surrealist Movement*, Thames & Hudson, London, 1975.

suggests, is what makes a woman strong and whole: it gives her a unique power to reach out to some greater totality – be it mankind, nature, or even the divine. Physically, this layering of experience is conveyed by correspondences between the senses, particularly sight, sound and touch; stylistically, by images that reflect one another, words and phrases that are repeated like a refrain or a litany. Every word is in place.

A year after publishing 'Les Jours de la femme Louise', *Les Temps Modernes* began to serialise *The Second Sex*, Simone de Beauvoir's momentous study of womanhood which, even if its mandarin tone grates a little today, marks the starting-point for the post-war feminist movement and remains perhaps its single seminal work. In the published book (1949) de Beauvoir refers to Madeleine Bourdouxhe's observation of the different value that is set upon the sexual act by women and by men.

> Madeleine Bourdouxhe tells of a woman who recoiled when her husband asked if she had enjoyed herself, putting her hand over his mouth; the expression horrifies many women because it reduces erotic pleasure to an immanent and separately felt sensation. 'Was it enough? You want more? Was it good?' – the very fact of asking such questions emphasises the separation, changes the act of love into a mechanical operation directed by the male. And that is, indeed, why he asks them. He really seeks domination much more than fusion and reciprocity.[5]

De Beauvoir was absolutely right to perceive that sexual polarity lies at the heart of Madeleine Bourdouxhe's work. In 'Anna', the most 'surreal' of the stories and the one that de Beauvoir probably had in mind, the bored wife of a garage owner wants to act, to start wars and revolutions, but she's trapped by her sex and her situation, and can only trace grand designs in the air above the marital bed. We are back in the world of fantasy. Anna dreams of a dress she doesn't possess, of a dance with another man that will liquefy her and raise her on a plateau above the world. She watches herself from inside her

5 *The Second Sex*, trans. H. M. Parshley, Penguin, Middlesex, 1972, pp. 417–18.

own body: she is both imprisoned in her flesh and liberated from it. In shocking, brutal imagery the clash of opposites lights up and subverts her everyday world. Looking at her own neck and breasts Anna thinks of her veins as pipes full of blood – and has a terrifying vision of it as coagulating, surging back to the heart. One is reminded of the Mexican painter Frida Kahlo Rivera's 'The Two Fridas', painted in 1939 during her divorce from Diego Rivera, in which imaginary pipes join two X-ray images of herself and blood courses from one heart to another, finally spluttering out on to a pure white dress.

'Anna' suggests that the image in the mirror must be questioned if the self is to be seen in all its complexity: as one is and as one might be, inside and outside of the body. And if the mirror exposes, that other tempting glass, the window, might help one escape into a better life – or, as in the haunting story 'Clara', whose protagonist's deafness is the ultimate symbol of non-communication, into death.

Not only for Clara is silence potentially both fatal and ideal. In 'A Nail, A Rose', the only story apart from *Sous le pont Mirabeau* to be based on Madeleine Bourdouxhe's own experience, Irene wanders alone in the snow and ice above the darkness of an occupied town thinking about her former lover. That they had no need of words, she realises, had become a cruel paradox, a mockery of silent communion, since all he could not tell her was that he had to leave her. (For another woman, or to work in the Resistance? She must not ask.) So when Irene is physically attacked from behind, the event is a brutal irrelevance, a momentary interruption of her continuing pain. Again, sexual differences are expressed in contrasting images: hard/soft, strong/weak, black/white. Irene cannot despise her attacker: he's too eager to please, like a child – out of work, maybe, or too young to fight – and they make friends; the Occupation seems to bind victim and attacker more than his violence separates them. She even feels compassion for him; nothing matters except the loss of her previous love. 'You mustn't take my little pleasures away from me,' she begs, when he tries to compensate for his brutality by offering to chop her wood.

Romantic love is all too easily dismissed, even by feminist critics, as the stuff of 'women's fiction'. Sometimes, as in the stories of Madeleine Bourdouxhe, it is gloriously that. The love that pours out here is of many kinds; not just sexual love but maternal love, parental love, men's love of women, women's love of men, women's love of women, love of animals, love of inanimate objects, spiritual love, the love you feel for a stranger (or a soldier). Love can be confining or it can be liberating – or it can be both. When a love affair ends or someone dies, the solitude can be wracking, as it is for Irene, or it can be the most desirable condition of all. In 'Blanche', described by its author as the 'lightest' of the stories, Blanche is driven almost to insanity by her crass, uncomprehending husband, finding more satisfaction in her relationship with the pots and pans in her kitchen than she could ever find with him; but escaping from home with her little son she finds solace in the stillness of the night forest and a fantasy lover – one of many in these stories – with whom no vows need be exchanged. Often in the work of Madeleine Bourdouxhe nightmares darken the light of day; here, ecstasy illuminates darkness.

Fantasy might save you from madness but it can also play up cruel contrasts. In the background of 'Leah', the long central story in *A Nail, A Rose*, there's an unnamed, absent traveller with whom Leah shares an obsessive longing for death: both are consumed by the 'slow impatience of time'. Leah's present reality, however, is the protective love she feels for an idealistic young factory worker, Carrol, who has fought in Spain; her environment is the shabby interior of the local café where men meet to banter and discuss revolt. But for all his talk, Carrol is afraid of the dark, so Leah must draw on her womanly strength and confront the forces of evil on his behalf; she must deal with the trouble-shooter who has caused his humiliation. Her task complete, she works like a professional, covering up her tracks, setting light to incriminating evidence. As she watches the hillside turning red, the biblical images of fire and blood that recur so frequently in these stories unite. Earlier, she felt 'a sorrowful love for the colour of blood'; now, 'the colour at the edge of the night was the only one [her] eyes could bear'. Her own hands are 'white and bloodless'. She might even have loved her lover's enemy in another life.

Finally, what happens when the fantasy world of *A Nail, A Rose* is inhabited not by a woman but by a man – in the case of

'René', a country boy who finds a vision of perfection in the lavender-scented hair of a marvellous stranger? Like the other men in the stories René drives himself to violence in his fury with the opposite sex, and the marvellous stranger only aggravates his mood by the passivity with which she receives his physical assault. Retreating to the small, domestic world from which all Madeleine Bourdouxhe's female protagonists have dreamed such powerful dreams, René remembers his victim as he left her: immobile, intact, eternal. She's a woman crucified alive. 'Did you notice that all my stories are about women – except for one?' Madeleine Bourdouxhe asked me with a penetrating look. She didn't elaborate. But it's just possible that this final image, in which gender is transcended and subverted at the same time, is the one with which she would like us to rest.

Faith Evans
February 1989

A Nail, A Rose

A Nail, A Rose

Walking through the streets, Irene could see no light. She passed other people on the pavements and in the streets, but couldn't see them either. All she could see was the image of Danny, picking up his glass in both hands and twisting it so that the beer swirled around in the bottom. He wasn't saying anything. Irene was talking and going slowly mad.

'There is something,' she had said, 'there is something you're not telling me . . . it might be something that you think is true but isn't at all . . . Tell me,' she said. 'Explain to me, speak, just speak to me . . .'

He hadn't answered; but then they weren't in the habit of explaining things to each other. That was how it was between them, they had no need of words. Then she'd said to herself that all she had to do was to walk out, all she had to do was to leave behind her, just as it was, this thing that she would never understand.

She could no longer remember whether she had said goodbye. She thought she hadn't; she thought she had just got up, walked across the room and opened the door. He didn't move or follow her. They were in the café where they often used to meet – the sign outside had the name of a flower on it, something like lily of the valley, or wallflower. It wasn't that she'd forgotten, but she always tried not to think of it. She walked into the street, but he didn't come after her, he didn't shout: 'Irene!'

She was walking in the dark roads. It hadn't happened that day, nor even the day before: it was a long time ago now. But ever since, whenever she walked through the streets, she always saw the same image, of Danny picking up his glass in both hands, swirling the beer at the bottom of it and saying nothing, whilst she talked and went slowly mad.

She was tired and the road was steep, so she waited at a tram stop. Sitting in the carriage, she closed her eyes, but images continued to assault her: his face, his hair, the hands she loved so much. Tears began to rise up through her body. She didn't like crying in the tram; it was much better to talk to yourself instead. Whatever it was, she would never understand it now . . .

Danny and Irene: that she did understand, she understood it perfectly, and she thought it meant she could understand the rest of the world as well: Danny and Irene, and the whole world. But she would never now understand the line that ran between them, like an arrow with a sharp point at either end. And the whole world was now this line.

Whenever they had met again after a parting, they had come together like two hands joining. They were like two hands of one being, finger against finger of the same length, palm against palm. And two hands of the same being are clasped together because of the same joy or the same agony. He didn't say, 'I love you,' and nor did she. Plenty of people say 'I love you,' but what existed between them wasn't the same as what exists between those people. Instead of saying 'I love you,' he said: 'Irene.' And she said 'Danny.'

Sometimes they were at the heart of love, like a bee in a closed flower. But only sometimes, because that wasn't the sole aim of their encounters. Two hands can join together in joy, in torment, in emotion, in prayer, or in revolt; but their love-making was a whole in which they touched on hope and despair. Because their love-making was savage and it was pure. They made love in heather, in orchards, in fields of cut corn; in bedrooms, too, and in other people's beds: that was their right.

When they made love the only words they spoke were 'Danny' and 'Irene'. Danny never gave her lilies of the valley, nor perfume, scarves or rings; his presents would be an ear of corn, a nail or a leaf. He sometimes gave her fruit; but not the sort of fruit that changes and turns putrid – the fruit that he gave her had hard, dry outlines and a fixed shape, like kernels.

She had got off the tram and was walking again, towards her house, in the slippery, deserted streets of the outskirts. A recent fall of snow, now half-melted, had been hardened by frost, and there were sheets of ice all over the place: she had to walk slowly. She could hear footsteps behind her, but they were some way away, and she paid no attention to them. A leaf, a nail, a kernel. How she had loved his hands, and his fair hair . . . in heather, in orchards, in fields of cut corn . . .

By now night had fallen, and the verges and the waste ground seemed to be etched in black and white: the only branches she could see were those on which snow was still lying. She was living through a present without a future, she was carrying inside her a love with no tomorrow. The world was empty, and she was walking along a road of hardened mud and snow.

It was a black night. In this year 1944 the darkness was total, the few houses that she passed black and dead. The road was deserted apart from those footsteps behind her; they were getting closer but still she paid them no attention. In heather, in orchards, in fields of cut corn . . . Now the man's footsteps were right behind her, he was close up to her, almost at her back, and he was hitting her on the head. Irene felt the blow while still lost in the memory of love. She turned round and saw a man wearing a cap, with a hammer in his raised hand.

'Take everything I have,' she said, 'just don't hit me any more.'

Her voice was choked. Could he hear what she was saying? She held out her handbag and case, but he didn't take them. His right hand was still raised, and with his left he grabbed the belt of her coat and held her close to him. She looked him full in the face – hoping to dissipate the feeling of vertigo brought on by his blows, and to banish the flame of pain that was dancing before her eyes. In the darkness she couldn't see the man's face clearly, but she felt that she could smell his body: she was soaking in his body smell.

'You're out of luck,' she said, 'you've wasted your time, attacking a woman with no furs or jewels . . . also, you're a lousy assailant – you're a fool, because if I'd started to cry out when you struck me so feebly, people would have come out of these black houses and run after you. There you are, have a look in there, take what interests you and leave me the rest.'

Still holding the hammer in his right hand, he let go of her coat and with his free hand took possession of the handbag and case.

'Oh no,' she said, 'you're not going off with the whole lot. What I said was that you could have a look at it all and that we'd divide it up. I didn't say you could take everything.'

'What are you going on about?'

'Don't shout so loud, someone might hear us.'

'That's true . . .'

'Let's sit down over there, on that bank. Have you got an electric torch?'

'Yes.'

'Put that hammer in your pocket, I don't like looking at it.'

'Are you frightened?'

'No, but I've been hurt. You hurt me.'

'Do you still feel bad?'

'I don't know . . . I don't care.'

'I'm going to tell you everything. Because you were moving, the hammer slipped, that's why I didn't hit you properly. What I really meant to do was to hit you bang on, on the top of the head.'

'Ping! with your metal hammer. That's a likely story!'

'Are you still afraid of my hammer?'

'No. Let's have a look at it.'

'Here.'

'It's really heavy . . . I had a narrow escape.'

'But tell me, what on earth were you up to, all alone in the dark?'

'I was just walking, walking and thinking.'

'What were you thinking about?'

'About my love life.'

'Do you mind if I look at you with the torch? . . . Yes, you're a lovely girl.'

'Present without future, a love with no tomorrow, an empty world. We can touch neither perfection or eternity.'

'What?'

'Nothing, I was talking to myself. So, are we going to divide up my fortune?'

'If you like. Let's have a look. A packet of cigarettes . . .

'That's for you.'

'Thanks. A lipstick . . . You can keep that.'

'Money – you take it,' she said. 'There must be about a hundred francs there. And there's another fifty francs in an envelope; here you are.'

'Thanks. A nail . . .'

'Yes, a nail.'

'A nail from a horse's hoof?'

'Yes, from a horse's hoof.'

'It's quite new, it's never been used.'

'No, it's never been used.'

'It's for you,' he said.

'Yes, it's for me.'

'Here you are.'

'Thanks,' she said. 'Listen, you own the cigarettes now – what would you say if we had a smoke?'

'Sure.'

All around them, the earth was black and white. A beautiful winter night-smell rose up from the black and white earth. A vast night meadow, the colour of the earth, flowed out before and beneath her, stretched to infinity, because the mass of the darkened town beyond it, sunk in the apathy of a town under Occupation, could not be clearly distinguished. From the heart of the town she expected there to rise the alarm of the sirens, she expected an anguish to be born that would rise up in sea-swells from the darkened town and unfurl over the fields, the countryside, the world. And she expected there to rise up at the same time a wave of mould that would swell and spread all over the world, and into her heart. The world is empty, and so is the sky, we can touch neither perfection nor eternity. But how beautiful the earth is, black with mud, white with frost. How beautiful it is, under its winter night-smell that rises from the earth, the trees, the air.

'Well then,' she said, 'shall we divide up my food coupons?'

'Yes,' he said. 'I'd be interested in those all right. Hey, you've got milk coupons – you have a kid?'

'Yes.'

'You're married?'

'Nothing to do with you.'

'But the kid . . .?'

'Given to me by the man I love. Will that do?'

'You've been lucky, then. Not everyone gets to have a kid by the man they love.'

'No, not everyone.'

'Kiss me.'

'If you like.'

'No, not like that. Kiss me properly.'

'If you like.'

'Come on, let me hold you close, in my arms.'

'No.'

'I only want to hold you close, in my arms. I won't do anything you don't want me to. I promise.'

'What would be the point? Why do you want to hold me close?'

'Because I didn't kill you.'

She got up and he held her against him for a moment, pressing his hands against her back. She could smell and feel his body, long and straight and smooth apart from two bumps in the middle – one inert (the head of the hammer which he had slipped into his pocket), the other very much alive. 'I'm going to faint,' she said. 'I'm surely going to faint . . . Please, let me get my breath. I'm not feeling too good.'

'What's the matter? Is your head hurting?'

'Yes, but it's not that. My heart's racing.'

'Did I hold you too tight? Have I done something to annoy you?'

'What an idea! Listen, try and take it in: you're walking along the street, you're seeing all sorts of things inside your head as you walk along, and someone comes up on you from behind and hits you on the head, suddenly, just like that. Wham! A shot in the back, from behind – it's revolting.'

She ran her hand over her face, her forehead, her whole head.

'Oh no,' she said. 'Let's have your torch.'

She held out her hand in the narrow beam of light. It was covered with blood.

He inspected her thoroughly with his torch: there was blood all over her hair and it was running on to her shoulders and coat.

'I didn't realise,' she said. 'Why didn't I feel it trickling down my neck?'

'Because your hair acted like a gutter.'

'You've done a great job, haven't you? You really are a swine.'

'Yes,' he said.

He got out his handkerchief and tried to clean her hair, to staunch the wound. She was standing up, her heart racing. A man was wiping blood from her hair – and although he was doing it gently, she was in pain. He was holding the torch on a level with their faces, and she could see his pale greyish skin and the lock of brown hair that fell on to his forehead. He'd pushed his cap back and his face looked young and very thin. It was the face of an archangel or a fool: that look could belong to either one or the other. Beyond the slope, the night fields stretched out, rejoined the horizon, rose up and reappeared in a dome above them, black from top to bottom. The earth was less black than the sky, with patches of ice criss-crossing it. The sky was empty; and she was in pain. At the corner of the road there rose up, like a miracle, a tree covered with hoar-frost.

'I ought to be getting back,' she said.

'I'll come with you for a bit,' he said. 'The roads aren't safe.'

He was still cleaning her up.

'All this blood,' he said. 'What are you going to tell them at home?'

'I'll say I slipped on some ice. I'll say I fell backwards, and that my head hit the pavement hard.'

'You came up with that one quickly – you're a pretty good liar, aren't you?'

'About my things, is there anything else that interests you?'

'No. Here, take your cigarettes.'

'No, you keep them.'

'I insist, take them back.'

'Aren't we polite to each other . . .'

'Tell me, where do you live?'

'Very near here. I'll be fine on my own now.'

'Who do you live with?'

'With my brother, my father, my father's four brothers and their six sons. If my brother saw you, he'd take hold of you and turn your body into a knot in one second flat. Have you seen that Charlie Chaplin film where the policeman bends street-lamps? He's a bit like him, my brother.'

'Are you teasing me?'

'I'm teasing you.'

'But seriously, where do you live?'

'Very near here. You'll be able to see me going in. Just stay where you are and let me go now. Goodbye . . .'

'Goodbye. What's your name?'

'Irene. And yours?'
'Jean.'
'Cheers, Jean.'
'Cheers, Irene.'

She went in without making the slightest sound. Half-opening the door of the bedroom she could see that Dan was asleep and so was Maggy, the kid who looked after him. She gently closed the door behind her and picked up a hand mirror. Standing in front of the looking-glass above the fireplace and holding the mirror behind her head, she tried to take stock. The lights were blacked out, which made it hard to see, so she struck a match and held it close to her head. That was no good because she had the mirror in one hand and the match in the other, and besides, she was too far from the looking-glass. Her hair was all stuck together at the roots: she really ought to wash it, and her scalp ought to have some stitches.

She called a doctor, but he lived too far away to come on foot, and didn't dare venture out by car because of the ice. Too bad – she hated having stitches anyway. She lay down on the bare floorboards, on her stomach, so as not to lean her head on the ground, and tucked her face inside her folded arms: that was the way to do it. Maggy had washed the floor, and it gave off the smell of damp wood. Inside her folded arms, she closed her eyes.

A nail from a horse's hoof . . . in bedrooms, too . . . in Lorraine, in the country I was chased from by the war. But the war is everywhere. In Lorraine there are towns covered with gold. It was in Lorraine, leaning against some flowers on a wall, that I said to you: 'If one day you no longer love me, you must tell me so.' Why did you swirl the beer in the bottom of your glass without saying anything? Why didn't you say anything when I said to you, 'Speak to me, speak to me,' whilst I was going slowly mad? In heather, in orchards, in ferns, in fields of cut corn . . . My too faithful memory has no future: it's closed to today, affirming and consuming itself at once. I live in the memory of a flower without a name. Oh my love, why did you abandon me? I live in the memory of a lost flower, I live in my devastated kingdom. And here I am inside my folded arms, hands clasped in anguish, while a vast mould spreads all over the world.

Next morning, the man came back, and stood waiting by the

garden fence. Irene went down to the gate and opened it.

'I'm not coming in,' he said. 'I've just come to find out how you are.'

'I'm better. It wasn't very serious.'

'I've brought you a bottle of milk and some porridge oats.'

'Thank you,' she said, 'but you shouldn't deprive yourself. What you took from me isn't going to put you back on your feet.'

'It's OK . . . since then, I've found what I was looking for.'

He reached out and felt her hair.

'Show me your head . . . Your hair is still all red.'

'It's not easy to wash out. Would you like a cig or two?'

'I sure would.'

He stayed by the gate while she went back into the house and came back with some cigarettes.

'Tell me, did you tell the police about me?'

'Are you daft or something?'

'Sorry. Look, here's my address.'

He held out a bit of paper.

'What could I do for you?' he asked. 'If there's anything you need doing around the house, you must drop me a line – if you've any wood that needs chopping, for instance, that sort of thing.'

'I like to chop my own wood. You mustn't take my little pleasures away from me.'

'All right. I'd like to give you a present. What would you like?'

'I don't like presents much . . .'

'Is there really nothing you want?'

'Oh I don't know . . . it's difficult to say.'

When he had gone, Irene stayed by the gate. What a strange episode, this man who'd not been afraid to return. Neither perfection nor eternity; some good, some evil. And while she waited, the mould was rising in layers, on the world and in her heart. Because of Danny. Why is it that we don't see each other any more, why do we no longer come together, like the two hands we once were? I'll never understand. 'I'd like to give you a present – what would you like?' A present for Irene . . .

The man had gone and she could answer now, since it was not him that she was answering.

'I'd like a rose of Jericho.'

Anna

Anna

'Come on,' he said, 'get some change . . .'

'All right,' Anna said.

She went in and returned with the notes. She watched Nicolas as he hung the hose back on the petrol pump and handed over the change; she watched the car as it pulled out, re-entered the right lane, and disappeared in the direction of Maisons-Alfort. At the garage over the way another car pulled in. The woman who worked there was tall, gaunt, older than Anna, and she wore an old-fashioned chignon on the crown of her head, fastened not with hairpins but with four or five criss-crossing nails, which formed a rosette around the chignon: a real curiosity.

Anna watched the woman as she served the petrol and hung the hose back on the pump. She watched the car as it pulled into the right lane and drove off in the other direction along the Maisons-Alfort road.

'How much longer are you going to stand around like that? What about some grub?' Nicolas shouted from the open window.

'Coming,' Anna said, 'coming.'

Anna leaned over the gas stove, holding two veal chops above the frying-pan without dropping them in. The meat beneath her fingers was as white and insipid as the cars that went by on the road to Maisons-Alfort. She chopped two onions and put them in the pan, then minced two cloves of garlic and added them with a sprig of thyme. As she waited for it to brown, she looked at the meat that she'd dropped on the paper. It was as insipid as the cars, or the smell of petrol that rose up around her the whole day long.

It's odd, Anna thought, how often you see garages at the cinema: there's been one in all the recent films I've seen. There was that garage where a man and a woman loved each other to distraction: then there was the one where a horrendous crime was being plotted, the one where an amazingly handsome man got stranded and then stayed on . . . and the garage that was started by a group of young people, where they all had a hell of a time . . .

It's not only what happens in a garage – there's something about the place itself, even about the quite simple objects that I see every day of my life. Somehow the pump, the garage sign and the end of the road all seem to be splashed with sun, and even when it's raining they glow, they glow so strangely. Oh yes, garages make a good setting for great crimes and great passions, all right . . . You can tell that these film producers don't live in a garage; if they came to visit they'd soon find out what goes on: absolutely nothing.

Anna walked into the glass porch holding the frying-pan.

'Shit, there's a customer,' Nicolas said.

He went out. Anna put the pan on the table and sat down. She could hear the noise of the pump and then a monkey-wrench being thrown on to the pavement. The meat was getting cold in the pan. Anna breathed a deep sigh, her white linen top stretching across the bosom, and lowered her head. Her bosom was beautiful, high and firm. She folded back the lapels of her top as far as her cleavage.

Anna's breasts were marked with white and blue lines: veins, she thought, pipes full of blood. For her, a breast could only be truly beautiful if it was made of marble, or of stone. It wasn't that blood frightened her – she didn't at all mind blood when it was red and flowing . . . Anna's thoughts always ran on ahead, and straight away she could see blood that was coagulated and blackened, blood that was decomposing, blood that surged back to the heart.

Nicolas came back and sat down again.

'Aren't you going to help yourself?' he said.

'I'm not hungry.'

Nicolas shrugged and took a veal chop.

'It's nice and tasty,' he said.

Anna cut herself a small piece of meat from the pan and chewed it, but it stuck in her throat.

'Nicolas,' she said, 'turn the radio off for a moment . . .'

'Why? It's a cheerful song.'

It was a cheerful song. Anna imagined a man on a motorbike. He was going fast, he hit a pole, his head hit the pole. She saw liquid, red blood surging back to the heart. The man was quite dead.

Anna was sitting slightly away from the table, but her hands were on it. 'Nicolas . . .' she said, in the way that people do when they mean, 'Help me . . .'

'Well, what is it?' Nicolas said, busy eating his meat.

'Oh, nothing.'

She walked over to the sink and swallowed a glass of water, then came back to the table and helped herself to some food. She ate her meat, just like Nicolas, just like everyone else.

'Is that all there is?' Nicolas said.

'There's some salad,' Anna said.

When they had eaten their salad, she cleared away and began to wash up. Nicolas had dozed off right there in his chair, his head cradled in his arms. He was tired; he had been late getting to bed the night before, because he had had to finish repair work on two cars that were being picked up early.

They heard a car hooting, repeatedly, outside the house.

'Go and see what it is, love,' Nicolas said in a sleepy voice.

'All right,' Anna said.

After pumping ten litres, Anna hung up the hose, took the money and watched the car leave. Car drivers were never interesting. They called out how many litres they wanted, paid, said thank you. Most of them didn't even get out of their cars: they left it to you to unscrew the cap and screw it back on again. Even when there was a repair to be done, the driver and his family stayed in their cars. When a vehicle had to be cranked up, they all got out and went off for a walk along the road, coming back when it was finished, saying thank you and driving off quickly so as to make up for lost time. With cyclists it was different: they had charm. The cyclist did the work himself and asked you to give him a hand, to hold the bike this way or that, and he talked to you while he was doing the job. When he'd finished, he'd mop his brow and say:

'It's hot, is there a café around here?'

'No,' Anna would say, 'but I can get you a glass of lemonade if you like.'

She'd go and get the bottle. By way of thanks, the cyclist would talk for a moment, tell her where he came from and where he was going. And when he left, Anna might gaze after him for a long time, still imagining him even when he had disappeared way up the road. Only very rarely did cyclists come to the garage.

Anna went back in to finish the washing up. The phone rang. It was in the glass porch, on the table which served as a desk. Anna heard Nicolas saying, 'Hello . . . Hello!' several times, and then: 'No one there.' He stretched out on the small sofa and went back to sleep while Anna put the cutlery and plates away and ran a cloth over the kitchen tiles. The phone rang again.

'Hello,' Nicolas said. 'Hello!' he yelled. He hung up, furious. 'Impossible to get back to sleep now . . .'

He went out, brought a wheel on to the pavement and started to repair it. Anna heard the thud of a tyre on the paving stones as the phone rang for the third time.

'Hello?' Anna said.

'It's Bobby. Would you like to come out with me in a bit?'

'Yes . . . yes,' Anna said.

'Come and pick me up, we'll go dancing.'

'Yes . . . yes.'

She hung up, took out her handkerchief and passed it over her lips, which were slightly moist. Nicolas climbed up the wooden stairs and came in.

'Who was that on the phone?'

'Bobby,' Anna said.

'Must have been that shithead who woke me up twice, then. He wants to take you out, doesn't he?'

'Yes . . .' Anna said.

Nicolas was holding a monkey-wrench in his hand and he slammed it down violently on the little table by the phone, turned his back on her and made for the door.

'Nicolas . . .' Anna cried, 'you know I won't do anything bad . . .'

'Do whatever you like, you really are a pain,' Nicolas said, banging the door.

Anna sat on the edge of the sofa, hands clasped tightly between her knees. Nicolas was livid; he didn't want her to go out with Bobby.

Anna's body was there on the sofa too – her hands, her knees, her arms. You couldn't say that her body was opposite her, because Anna was inside her own body, she actually was this body full of veins, these veins full of blood. And yet these veins and this blood nauseated her, made her sick at heart.

Was she really nothing but this body that made her so uneasy? And what function did it serve? If, for example, Anna thought, a woman carrying a pail full of rubbish were to get a little graze on her hand, and the dirt from the rubbish were to penetrate the graze and mingle with the dirt in her body, the scratch would swell up and redden, the body would become diseased and gangrenous, and the woman would die.

Anne could see the woman from the garage over the way, the woman with nails in her hair. She saw her pumping petrol – why? – with the hand that might have that graze on it. Not worth fussing about, she thinks, but then she catches cold, a bad dose of flu, and that's enough. It's no great loss: of what use was her old and ugly body? She might as well die straight away, get it over with. It was different for Anna: she was pretty, and younger. Several years younger, in fact.

What did they stand for, those years? Take a span of ten years, for instance. Ten years ago, she was pregnant with Paul; but time had passed so quickly since then that it seemed like yesterday. Anna could see herself as she was then, belly enormous and face puffy. There had been a time, then, when her body had not disgusted her. She used to run her hand over her swollen belly, her stretched skin; her body was distorted but she accepted it, because all of a sudden it had a clearly defined purpose, a real function. She had cared for Paul and suckled him, without thinking of anything else. Time had passed. It was a good time: she'd been creating Paul.

Now she wondered: what had been the point of it? She didn't know. It was Paul's business; let him fend for himself now. Anyway, she had enjoyed creating him. Paul wasn't there at the moment: he was nine now, and it was the holidays, so he was at his aunt's little farm near Chevreuse. He could manage without her now.

Anna sat there on the sofa, contemplating herself, her body. It wasn't that she had nothing to do all day, what with helping Nicolas - serving customers, preparing meals, doing the shopping, washing up, polishing, brushing, washing clothes, mending linen, cleaning Nicolas's suits. But all these things were done and then undone one by one. Washing up wasn't at all the same thing as creating Paul. She sat there on the sofa, next to the radio and the two tables - the one where they ate and the one which served as a desk - and in the midst of chairs, vases and other objects. Anna heard the cars passing by on the road to Maisons-Alfort, she heard the noise of the pump, the tyres and the monkey-wrenches on the paving stones, and she smelled the petrol. Objects, smells and noises into which her thoughts escaped, leaping over and ahead of them, beyond objects, hours, and days.

Through the window-pane - this place is all window-panes, she thought - Anna saw the woman from over the way, and a man who always turned up at this time and stopped either on the pavement opposite or on this one, according to the position of the sun and his desire for heat or shade. The man parked himself there because of the cars that pulled in. His cap would shake as he held it out, because he had a nervous disease. When he stopped walking, the tips of his toes stayed on the ground but his heels came and went, shaking his whole body. His left hand shook his outstretched cap and his right arm was bent back towards his shoulder, so that it seemed as if his open hand was forever in the act of greeting someone.

It was not good luck for Anna to have someone like that before her eyes: the road was saturated with the sun, heating the man's body and making the nails in the woman's hair glisten, while cars and motorbikes spun past, forever buzzing the silence. She closed her eyes and saw, just as if she really was seeing it, a motorbike coming at full speed, mounting the pavement over the way, flattening the woman with the chignon. Blood squirted all over the place, in streams and in showers, spilling out and coating everything: the pumps, the paving stones, the walls, the beggar, the entire road.

'You must understand,' Anna said. 'The woman over the way was completely flattened, just like that . . .'

Who was she talking to? 'You must try and understand,' she

cried out, 'you must try and understand these thoughts I have . . .'

Who was it in front of her that she was shaking like this with her outstretched hands, who was it that she was shaking so as to make him really understand her? It was probably Nicolas, who at this moment was repairing his wheel at the foot of the wooden staircase. Anna leaned over towards the window and looked out at the pavement. Nicolas was crouching down, his knees wide apart, slowly inspecting the tyre. He was furious with her, yet she loved him; she loved no other man. But being with Nicolas was just like being with the two tables, the sofa and the radio: she was imprisoned within her own body. Did Nicolas think that if she went out with Bobby it was to flirt or make love with him? None of that interested her. Love, it's all the same in the end – it never offers anything new. And as for the real thing, well, she'd never come across it, either in herself or in other people. Poor Nicolas, thinking that the fact that she liked going out with Bobby had something to do with going to bed . . . She couldn't explain to Nicolas why she liked going out with Bobby. The moment she began to explain it, it would sound daft.

Bobby said, 'OK, shall we dance? Lift up your train, princess.' They danced, far apart from each other, arm upon arm, graciously. And Anna's body slowly became transformed. She became so light that her body disintegrated and abandoned her; it was chased away, obliterated by the notes of music falling like rain and by the slow, gracious, distant movements of their arms. Bobby's face was before her. It was a face without wrinkle or blemish, and it seemed transfixed, as though it was no more than two clear eyes beneath black curly hair, eyes that were clear and powerful like a guardian angel's. And Anna, liberated from her body, was no more than a slippery, insinuating breath of air, a wide-eyed star, newly born and apprehending things and men and women and trees as if for the first time. For they were in the light now, not in the opacity of Anna's body but in the real light of the breath that she had become.

Bobby took her by the hand and led her between the tables and into the garden, then guided her to the room where the music came from. Standing next to each other, Bobby and Anna raised their glasses and gently clinked them. The *vin rosé* that they were drinking slipped down their throats, between breaths, all by itself, and the rain of music turned into hot, burning drops, burning to a cinder everything in her that was not breath. Anna was no more than dreams and vapours: she was vaporous, floating and reclining on a current of air. Gliding, buoyed up by the air, she could see things from higher up: she leaned over attentively, always waiting, always ready for the miracle that was going to be revealed, for the secret that was slowly to disclose itself, like a flower that half-opens to show the earth's sense of time, and the purpose of blood, and the meaning of truth.

One evening in Meudon woods she'd been with a man. Never mind whether he was called Bobby or something else: he had no name and Anna, a breath without a body, was no longer herself. She'd been lying on the ground with the man across her body, her arms stretched out and the man's arms on hers, and their hands were clasped together. She felt no physical longing as she lay there; eyes wide open, she was staring at the leaves of the tree above them and, beyond the tree, at the sky, all lit up with stars. And lying there on her back, quite flat on the ground and the earth, her eyes on the sky, Anna was thinking – as if she were expressing herself in words, though she wasn't – 'I am lying with this man next to me. It is me lying here, and at the same time I am outside myself; it's as if I am watching myself. I see a man and a woman lying down. They are silent, immobile, transfixed, and they will stay that way even when our hands disentangle themselves and our movements return to normal. They will stay like that now and for centuries to come, like marble or stone, touched with the miracle of grace. I can see them. And if someone is watching the earth from the highest star of all, this is how they will look: like marble or stone. And this is how they will be, a man and woman without names, eternally visible, superbly beautiful, like marble and stone. They will be the only people left on earth, and they will be of the earth.'

'OK, shall we dance? Lift up your train, princess.'

Sitting on the edge of the sofa, her hands clasped between her knees, Anna could hear Bobby's voice, and now she could hear the songs and the music, all hot and violent, so that, almost vaporous herself, she became heat and violence too. She got up and stood quite still, picturing herself enveloped by the folds of a much-loved dress. It was very long, this dress – it enveloped her completely – and was so full that it completely obliterated all the natural lines of her body. The material would hide her arms, and flowers would cover the fine blue lines of her breasts. But Anna didn't really have a dress like this, so she would wear her light grey suit and her cherry-red blouse.

She went to the hanging wardrobe, took out the grey skirt, brushed and ironed it. She washed her cherry-red blouse, hung it in the sun and ironed it when it was still damp. And while she was washing and ironing, she brushed and ironed a suit of Nicolas's, and washed a pair of his socks. Then she peeled some potatoes.

Anna went out to the forecourt two or three times to serve petrol. In the glass porch she laid the table, put on the grey suit and cherry-red blouse, and did her hair. Her hair was so fine that it never took to artificial waves but fell back naturally on to her forehead and face. Now she could hear the music inside her, now she was light and hot like a rain of music. When Nicolas came into the porch this was how he saw her, all dolled up and vaporous.

'So, you've decided to go out after all?'

'Yes, Nicolas . . . I'm going out . . .'

He moved close to her, very firm on his feet, his enraged face raised to hers:

'And what if I don't like it, you going out like this?'

All dolled up, and already vaporous, with a smile that was no longer hers, a smile that was immutable as a sigh, her head full of song, distant and invulnerable, Anna replied:

'But I am going out, Nicolas . . . Because Bobby asked me to . . . because he's expecting me . . .'

She didn't move, she stayed right there next to him, transfixed and smiling.

'I'll teach you to smile like that,' Nicolas said. He raised his fist and hit her bang on the corner of her mouth. Anna's smile disappeared in a star of blood.

Nicolas left the room, slamming the door behind him. Leaning over the basin, Anna washed her mouth with a flannel. Her teeth hurt. In the mirror, she could see the cut on her lip and the blood dripping from her exposed flesh: it trickled down again as soon as she wiped it off. She went and sat on the sofa, the flannel pressed against her mouth.

*

Anna stood up and went back to the mirror. She was no longer bleeding, but her lip was violet-coloured and swollen. In her head, in her heart, and all around her, there was a heavy void. She really was this body of hers, she really was this lip of hers; in fact she was no more than this lip of hers which, as soon as she moved it, began to ooze blood. She passed her tongue lightly over it.

She went down the wooden staircase and on the forecourt met Lucien, the young man who sometimes helped Nicolas out.

'I've come to stand in for Nicolas,' he said. 'He's gone shopping.'

'I see,' Anna said.

'What on earth have you been up to?' Lucien asked. 'Have you hurt yourself?'

'Yes, just now,' Anna replied. 'I missed a step and smashed my teeth against a water jug I was carrying.'

'You ought to put some arnica on it,' Lucien said.

Anna walked along the road; she walked for a long time, not knowing where she was going. Cars flew past in both directions. Turning off left into the narrower streets, she passed a café which had a little garden with two iron tables and some chairs. She turned back on herself, went into the little garden and sat down at a table. A cement wall, running at an angle to the house, closed off one side of the garden. There was a woman standing there, splayed against the grey wall, arms spread out, her skinny body enveloped in a black apron, her red hair against the grey wall. Some straggling, unhealthy vine-shoots clung to the wall to the right of the red-haired woman; a little above her bowed head there clustered, more vivaciously, the half-opened blooms of three passion flowers. Immobile, full of heat, the woman sighed as she leaned against the wall.

It was only early evening, but the heat was fierce, almost stormy. So hot was it that the tiny blooms of a virginia creeper, which formed an arch above Anna's table, exploded, and the seeds fell down in a fine rain, with a noise like fine rain, on to the table and into her hair. The seeds fell like rain, like green rain, hot, violent, impossible rain in the here and now where she could not be. She was inside her own body; she was nothing other than her own body; and yet it had no purpose. And this green rain was nothing either; it gave her nothing. It fell on her body, which was nothing other than her body, which was nothing either. Hot, violent, impossible rain; green rain which was not her rain. Rain, rain, green rain.

'I'd like a lemonade, please,' Anna said.

The red-haired woman came towards her, leaving the grey wall suddenly empty. She brought a bottle and a glass and placed them on the table in front of Anna.

'Forty sous,' she said.

The woman dragged herself, heavy with heat, to a table opposite Anna and sat down, her arms stretched out on the table, her hands playing with a key.

In front of the house two children were talking and shrieking with delight. 'Time to go in,' the woman shouted to them. 'You ought to be in bed.' The children went in by the back door and Anna could hear them still talking and laughing inside the house. They came into the little garden, making for the road.

'I told you it was time for bed,' said the woman.

Breaking into a run, the children carried on towards the road.

Anna looked at the children, then at the woman, and smiled at her. It hurt her to smile, and she dabbed at her lip with her handkerchief.

'They're not mine, they're my brother's children,' the woman said casually.

A strange smell was coming from the house, a bit like burning leather. Looking tense, the woman got up and sniffed the air.

She reappeared holding an odd-looking bunch of smoking rags.

'Filthy kids,' she said. 'Filthy bloody kids. They found a nest of mice – wrapped them up in my scarf – put them in the corner of the stove, the place where it gets really hot.'

She knelt down in the little garden, unfolded the smoking scarf and smothered it with her hands. The tiny little animals, pale pink and furless, crawled about on the ground letting out anguished squeaks. She took them by the tail and after bashing each one with a stone, stood up and kicked the whole lot into the hedge. Exhausted, she took up her place against the grey wall. The three passion flowers rediscovered their true purpose, their blooms posing and clustering around her as if to root her and make her universal, reaching into the heart of her and beyond.

Anna stayed still, her eyes fixed on the red-headed woman. Green rain fell on to the table, into her glass, on to her hair.

At last she got up, moved round the table and started to walk, heavy with heat. Back on the Maisons-Alfort road she retraced her steps: it was getting darker all the time but it was as hot as ever. She climbed the wooden staircase and sat on the sofa, her hands clasped between her knees.

When Nicolas came back he saw her sitting there, as if she hadn't moved.

'You didn't go out, then?' he said. 'You're still here . . .?'

He put his hand on her shoulder.

'Did I hurt you?' he asked.

'No,' she said.

'I get violent, I know . . . but it's just the way I am,' he said. 'Will you forgive me?'

Anna didn't speak or move so he said, 'OK, are we going to eat?'

She got up and went into the kitchen to heat some soup. Nicolas turned the radio on to listen to the news.

After the meal, Anna didn't say anything or clear away: she just sat there, as if numb. Nicolas drew the curtains across the glass partition, and said, 'Come on then, get your clothes off, let's get some sleep.'

He went on talking as he sat on the sofa removing his shoes: 'Hope there aren't any customers tonight.' He said 'tonight' from the bottom of his throat as if he were choking.

Under the quilt Anna was lying on her back, her arms tight against her body. Nicolas switched off the light and then, after tossing about a bit in the bed, turned towards her.

'You're not cross with me, are you? Are you?'

Nicolas was a big man: he shook the whole bed. He leaned heavily against her and his voice went soft. Whenever he spoke intimately he faltered and stammered: 'M-my d-dear little p-pussy . . .' Anna struggled: she was soaked in sweat and gasping, trying to keep her teeth clenched. She struggled against herself: Nicolas would overcome her body, and her body would overcome her. She was going to be transmuted, to turn into a piece of flesh, that would open like a flower. My God, she thought, I do not want that . . . transmuting, sliding, falling, my flesh opening like a flower . . . She was no more than a big rose-window, bulging and swollen: a rose-window from which she would eventually spring, re-formed, herself again.

Anna was weeping.

'What's the matter,' Nicolas said, 'are you crying? Your trouble is, you've been getting too much . . .'

My God, he was going to say the word. Anna put her hand on his mouth.

'I don't like that word,' she said.

'I'll have to watch it, then.'

He turned over in the bed, settled himself, and went on:

'Don't understand tarts . . . you try to give them pleasure and all they do is snivel. They're always crying – but they're not the ones who have to make war and revolution . . .'

'Maybe you're lucky to have the opportunity to do those things,' Anna said.

'Some luck . . . that's not what I call luck.'

'It's a challenge,' Anna said.

After a short silence she went on:

'You might be able to feel that you were really doing something useful, you might be able to do something for . . .'

She raised her hand, and to complete her thoughts traced a great circular shape in the darkness with an open and caressing movement.

'What are you drawing?' Nicolas asked.

'I'm chasing a fly,' Anna said.

Nicolas fell asleep. Anna kept her eyes open in the darkness of the bedroom. The glow from the illuminated pumps shone through a slit in the curtains and played on the blankets at her feet. It was dark outside but she could see the forecourt tinged with a sunless daylight, as if the day was already beginning. She could see the woman whose hair was punctured by nails and the figure of the man with his little arm folded back, his hand open: 'Greetings, greetings,' said the jerking beggar again and again . . .

Anna closed her eyes. It was springtime all over the earth. In a great green land, soldiers marched along a road past flowering orchards. The light smelled sweet, and immobile children looked into the soldiers' friendly faces. A woman raised her hand: 'Good day, soldiers.' Two women raised their hands: 'Will you be coming back this way?' The soldiers were singing, the songs they sang all week and on Sundays too: regimental tunes, waltzes, romantic songs. Every single note rent the air, calling up all the words in the world and unveiling eternity to the hearts of the dying.

Anna could see the men's friendly faces and the flowering orchards. She was neither the child nor the woman who had greeted them: she was the song that the soldiers were singing.

Louise

Louise

When melted sugar falls on to the steel surface of a stove it's the very devil, it sticks like glue. To get it off you need steel wool and an emery cloth. Holding the cloth with both hands, Louise rubbed to and fro with all her strength. Her hair fell over her eyes; she pushed it away with the back of her blackened hand. She stopped for a moment to catch her breath and looked at herself in one of the glass panes of the wardrobe: because of the curtain on the inside, the pane acted as a mirror. Louise was pleased by her reflection. She feigned a smile and opened her mouth a fraction, revealing a missing tooth, high up on the left: a shame, but fifty francs to replace. She went back to scrubbing the stove; again, her hair fell into her eyes. Louise: small, skinny, full of grace.

She went to fetch a box of vegetables and began to peel some potatoes. The ground-floor doorbell rang; she opened the window and leaned out.

'Odette, I'm throwing the key down.'

She went out on to the landing and listened to Odette coming up the stairs.

'Have you been good at school?'

She smoothed Odette's hair and straightened her headband.

Louise went back to peeling potatoes. Odette picked up the peelings as they fell on to the table and cut them into miniscule pieces, then put them into tidy little heaps.

'Are we going to have chips, Mama?'

'We'll have whatever Madame asks us to make.'

'I'll tell her I like them, then she'll say yes.'

'You will not, Odette, I forbid you to mention it.'

Odette picked up a cup, crammed it full of peelings, took it to the sink and turned on the tap. Water squirted out, spattering the furniture, the table, everything within range.

'Yes, I will say it. And I know she'll tell you to do chips.'

Louise turned round and quickly smacked her.

'I forbid you to mention it. And you're making everything dirty. As soon as you turn up you stop me doing my work.'

Odette was surprised by the blow; she raised her arm to shield her face. Louise caught her by the wrist, shook her, and slapped her again. Just at that moment, Madame opened the door.

'Come here, Odette, I've got some pictures for you to look at. You're getting on your mother's nerves in here.'

Madame spoke in her calm voice. She took Odette out of the room quietly, exactly as she had entered it.

Louise went back to work and thought about Madame. Madame was gentle; she said little, and there was nothing to add to what she said.

Now she had to wash the vegetables. It wasn't an unpleasant task: your hands were in nice cold water and the sink was near the window, so you could watch the street while you were at work. It was a beautiful sunny day and Louise wished she could be out walking. She would be doing that tonight, when she'd finished work, when the kid was asleep. She'd walk along the street, confidently; she'd walk into a café and have a drink, for seventy-five centimes; she might even run to one franc twenty-five and sit at a table. She liked to do that: she liked to be in a place where people were enjoying themselves. Occasionally men would come and talk to her, and some of them were nice. When Louise knew that she could go out in the evening, she thought about it all day long. It was her only form of entertainment, but there was more to it than that – it was a haven, a reassurance, and she was surrounded by people.

It was October and the evenings were fresh; she'd look ridiculous in a cotton dress. What she needed was a light coat, in blue cloth perhaps, with a round collar, buttoned from top to bottom, to hide the shabby dress beneath. Yes, a round cloth collar, perhaps with another one pinned on top of it, in white rep. She'd put lipstick on, she'd do her hair properly, and what with the blue coat as well she'd look really pretty. A man might come and sit at her table: Bob, for instance. She would be wearing her coat and she would run into Bob.

But what was she doing dreaming like this? For a full ten minutes her hands had lain still on the vegetables in the water. Her hands were very cold, and now they were also very clean; the water had made them smooth. They were a bit red, perhaps, but that would pass. They looked even better now than they did after she'd done the washing. That made them clean but wrinkled. Louise got back to work, chopped the vegetables and threw them into the pot.

Madame came back, with her gloves on, ready to go out. While she gave Louise some instructions about lunch, Odette stood very close to her, clinging to her, pawing her coat with the grubby hands of a child who is never completely clean. Louise said:

'You'll mess up Madame's clothes.'

Madame neither agreed nor disagreed, but as she continued talking she put her arm round Odette and kept her close. Louise didn't dare say any more. As soon as Madame had left, Odette said:

'You see, I didn't say anything about the chips.'

She smirked, bent her knee, held her foot in both hands behind her back, and hopped up and down on the other. She held her skinny, dirty, pathetic little face up to her mother. It was a pointed face, paler than Louise's but with many of the same fine features, like the big black eyes that had a fiery, almost feverish look about them.

Louise moved towards her child and embraced her too tightly.

'Off you go now . . . Go and look at your pictures.'

Louise went back to the sink. From the window she could see Madame walking along the street. She'd dressed up nicely: she'd put on her three-quarter-length coat. It was a blue coat with a round collar. Madame walked with verve and elegance. Louise could make her out less clearly now: she was getting hazy, mingling with the crowd. She spotted her one last time before she disappeared altogether. She carried on watching, without thinking, as if in a trance, and as she stared out of the window into the street a whole series of images of Madame came into her mind. She saw her in the morning when Louise arrived, saying in her soft and special voice, 'Good morning, Louise, how are you?' Madame never said anything when work was done badly – she just looked amused, raised her eyebrows and pointed at the trail of dust under the table. When that happened, there was nothing for it but to go and fetch the broom and start the work all over again. At times like that Louise was never tempted to answer back or offer excuses. The long trail of dust seemed to her to be something abnormal that had been grafted on to the world, something totally outlandish that could not be allowed to stay there for a moment longer.

Next Louise saw Madame coming home and asking in a strange breathless voice, 'Did anyone telephone?' At other times Madame would look down at Louise's hands with a look that was even stranger than her strange voice and say, 'No letters?' Faced by empty hands and a negative answer, her manner would change. You couldn't say that she seemed sad or disappointed, exactly: the words 'sad' and 'happy' were not words that you would apply to Madame. You could only say that she had this or that look on. Louise called this one her 'phone call and letter' look. But what phone call, what letter was it she was waiting for? Nothing ever came. When she looked like this you might well imagine that she had a lost child. It was always hard to know much about other people, but of Madame it was quite impossible to know anything at all.

Then she saw Madame that day when she'd been ironing some linen on the kitchen table, and Louise, who was right next to her, had raised her eyes, looked Madame straight in the face and said, 'You know, it comes through in your face how clever you are . . .' Madame had laughed openly at Louise's admiration. She was holding a damp ribbon in her hand and as she spread it out on the edge of the table to remove the creases, she stopped laughing and said, as if confiding something to herself, 'Intelligence is one thing, but "that" is quite another.' 'That'? What did she mean? Louise didn't understand. But there were so many things about Madame she didn't understand that this 'that' simply stood for all the incomprehensible things rolled into one. Madame was intelligent, and what's more she was 'that'.

There was also Madame's beauty, the beauty she had shown

just now, when she opened the door of the kitchen and when she walked along the street. With other women you could say where their beauty came from – from their big eyes, their well-shaped mouth or their wavy hair. Madame did have beautiful eyes, mouth and hair but it wasn't because of any of these that she was beautiful. What was it then? Was it 'that'? Oh it's too difficult, you go round and round in circles. Louise meant to get back to work and she moved away from the window – but she instantly returned to it to spend one last moment staring out into the street, brooding on the beauty which she could not explain, on what Madame had said whilst ironing the ribbon and on how little she knew about her. Louise thought of a simile which pleased her. She turned it over in her mind a few times and then said it out loud: 'Madame is as beautiful as a mystery.'

A little comforted by this, Louise left the window, filled a bucket with hot water and got down to work.

Madame came back. Everything happened so quickly that Louise went on feeling bewildered for some time afterwards. She admired Madame's coat and asked, 'Was it expensive?' Madame laughed, and Louise apologised for the question, explaining how much she would like a coat like that.

'Well then, Louise, I'll lend it to you for your evening off tonight.'

Louise protested; later she forgot exactly how. Madame laughed again and helped her into the coat.

'You're smaller than me, so it becomes a full-length coat rather than a three-quarter one, that's all. It suits you very well.'

Louise did remember saying:

'Madame, you're not like other people . . . It's not normal, you lending your coat to someone like me . . .'

'I don't need it tonight, and you really want it. What would be abnormal would be not to lend it to you.'

And as always, Louise could find nothing to say.

Now she was standing there, the coat folded over her arm, ready to go home. Odette asked:

'Are you taking Madame's coat away with you?'

Again Louise was struck by the oddness of the situation. As she took the child away she replied, 'Yes, I'm going to strengthen one of the seams.'

*

Louise and Odette ate their supper side by side – bread and ham – and drank their glass of red wine. Still eating, Odette leaned her head against her mother's arm and said, 'Would you like some of my orange, Mama?'

'No.'

'Yes!'

'Just a quarter then.'

Louise cleared the table, undressed Odette and put her to bed. She waited a little while until the child fell asleep and then, walking on tiptoe, crossed the bedroom to the wash basin. She combed out her pretty brown hair, rolled some strands up into little curls and piled them on top of her head in the fashionable manner. She had no rouge for her cheeks but she did have a lipstick, so she rubbed some of it between her fingers and expertly applied it to her skin. Hair done and face made up and powdered, she put the blue coat back on again. There are small moments of happiness in life that can, briefly, give as much joy as the greatest of miracles.

Louise couldn't see all of herself in the glass above the wash basin so she stood on a chair, where she could see everything from her hips to her ankles. The bottom of the coat billowed out slightly, and hung like a dream, just over her knees. She walked out of the bedroom, turning the key in the door without a hitch.

The city was all lit up, and Louise walked along feeling very happy. She stopped in front of one café but didn't go in, then in front of another, but still she walked on. In this evening full of lights she was searching for something, but she didn't know what it was.

She made for an area that she knew and went into her usual café. She went up to the bar and asked for a coffee. There was a man there, absurdly got up, who was going from café to café: he was carrying an instrument made out of a wooden pole and a sardine-tin which he was pretending was a violin, miming the movements and imitating the sound with his lips. He wore a tiny green silk hat, and this hat was connected by a small rubber tube to a squeezer concealed in his pocket. Whenever the man pressed the squeezer the hat shot up in a crazy way. Everyone burst out laughing when that happened and so did Louise.

The clown left the café but the jolly atmosphere lingered. Louise sat down at a table and ordered a glass of cider, drinking it in tiny sips, watching people coming in and out. From behind the bar, the waiter called out to her: 'You look smart tonight!' She gave him a big smile, which faded very slowly. She drank a little more cider. Minutes passed, more and more slowly, and time began to drag. It must be lovely to wait when you know that someone is going to turn up, Louise thought to herself. Lowering her head, she went off into a sort of dream. She felt very pretty and very alone.

The coat gave off a faint whiff of something – a mixture of perfume and body smell, as if the material was still warm from a skin that had just left it. In the place where her own heart was beating, another heart had recently beat too. 'Oh, how good she is to me,' she nearly said out loud. No one else would have offered to lend a garment like that. She is so good, so beautiful ... These were the only two adjectives Louise could find, but she knew that there ought to be other words to use and she would have liked to know them.

Closing her eyes, Louise summoned up Madame's image again, for it seemed to her that this was the best way to find the right means of describing her. She concentrated on thought rather than expression. She saw her with all her distinctive features: the long thoughtful face, the forehead that was almost too high, the smile, the fingers so slender that rings slipped about on them, the beautiful, rather tired eyes whose gaze penetrated the meaning behind every action. If only this passing time was being killed waiting for her. To be her friend, or rather her sister – that surely would be the happiness of a lifetime. If only she were to come into the bar, sit down at her table, and say, 'Why are you so unhappy, Louise?'

'I'd not be so unhappy if Bob loved me just a little.'

'You mustn't be unhappy, Louise – you know that *I* love you.' They would leave together, and talk, and have no secrets from one another.

But it wasn't like that. Louise was alone. She had a daughter; but though a child might give warmth, a presence and a reason for living, she couldn't offer relief or help of any kind – she was more like a tender burden.

Louise left the bar and walking smartly made her way towards the market area of Les Halles, where Bob usually hung out.

Today she would dare to go and look for him, because today she was much too pretty for him to reject her.

She went first into one café, then into another, and a third. Each time she walked straight out again, because Bob wasn't there and no one had seen him that evening. At last someone was able to tell her something: Bob had just gone out with the café owner and he'd be back soon. Louise sat down at a table to wait for him.

And when Bob did come back, she didn't move; she made no sign.

He stood at the bar with some of his mates. She took a piece of paper and a pen out of her bag and began to write down some figures, as if she was deep in an important calculation. Instead of the figures that she was writing at random, Louise wanted to write 'Bob' – or rather, 'Bob, I love you,' – but she didn't dare because she was afraid that he might suddenly come up to her table. She went on writing random figures. And then, as if it was moving by its own impetus, the pen traced an 'M', a very small 'M', on the corner of the paper. It went back over the letter several times, pressing down hard, adorning it with flowery bits and surrounding it with little marks which might have been stars or perhaps flowers, though they didn't particularly look like either. In the end, beneath her sums the whole corner of the paper was filled up. It became a cabalistic message of love.

Louise waited. Time didn't weigh so heavily any more; it could stretch out a bit longer yet, because at the end of all this waiting there might be tenderness and joy.

Bob turned round and looked at her. 'You writing to your lover? Is he dark or fair?'

She greeted him casually and said, 'No, I'm doing my accounts.'

He picked up his glass, put it down on the table and sat down opposite her. He gave a little whistle of admiration. 'Hey, you're all dolled up tonight . . . you look really good.'

She said mockingly, 'Do I really?'

'I just said so, didn't I?'

The other men finished their drinks and left. Bob let them go and stayed on with Louise. With all the restraint she could muster she managed not to reveal how happy this made her. He asked: 'Shall we go and have some onion soup?'

She pretended to think about it before saying, 'All right, if you like.'

At the bistro they were sent up to the first floor.

'That's smart,' Bob said, laughing.

The first floor was a very small room right at the top of the stairs, with three wooden tables covered with paper cloths. Louise went over to sit by the window. Just as Bob was about to sit down he adopted a mock gallant air and said, as a joke:

'Will you parmit me, Meddem . . .?'

Louise laughed softly. She was no longer concealing her joy: she let her happiness shine out of her face, her voice, and her eyes, which looked tenderly at Bob. He was wearing his work jacket, his hair was uncombed and he hadn't shaved, but untidiness suited him: he was young and strong, with a good complexion and physique, and he could get away with anything. The soup was good and hot and they ate with pleasure.

A dog appeared at the top of the stairs, hesitated, and went back down. Louise guessed that this must have been the animal that had recently deposited a little pile under a nearby chair. From where he was sitting, Bob couldn't see it. She started to laugh. She didn't dare tell Bob why, but the idea that she was laughing because of a little pile of dog-shit made her laugh all the more. The laughter was uncontrollable and Bob, thinking she was laughing for no reason, caught it too. They laughed together, louder and louder, every now and again saying they must calm down but then starting again all the louder. Finally Bob said:

'Wow, that makes you thirsty . . .'

He ordered a bottle of red wine: if they went on like this, they'd get through ten francs' worth. They started to laugh again at the very idea. Bob was hot and he took off his jacket. He was wearing a dark blue short-sleeved shirt with a turn-down collar buttoned at the neck – no tie. One button was missing. Louise hadn't removed her coat and she'd eaten carefully, with her left hand spread open on her chest like a napkin.

Bob paid for the soup and the wine. When they were downstairs Louise bought a bag of chips from the stall in front of the bistro. They walked along eating them, side by side. How lovely and fine it was out of doors! Better than earlier on, or so it seemed to Louise.

When all the chips were eaten, Bob put his arm round Louise and pushed her into the corner of a doorway, up on to a step so that her eyes were almost on a level with his. He kissed her gently, and then looked into her eyes. She said, 'My love . . .'

Her voice was fainting, and full of tenderness. She left her mouth half-open and Bob kissed her again.

Then he led her away, holding her round the hips and lifting her up a little.

The deep sleep of an exhausted woman is not interrupted by dawn. Only the loud noises of morning – the thud of empty dustbins chucked back on to pavements, the honking of the first buses – could wake Louise from her stupor.

She pulled the blankets up to her shoulders and remained in that position, feeling strangely sad. Bob wouldn't come back this evening; it would be days and days before he came back, maybe a whole month even. And to have left her in the street like that, so abruptly, without a kiss, without a word . . . It is not one of those things that you can be sure of, but she had a feeling that this behaviour was proof that Bob didn't love her. But didn't she know that already, that Bob didn't love her? How much did it matter?

Louise shrugged her shoulders under the blankets, then turned round so that her face was on the pillow. She felt like nothing.

Why aren't you my friend, she thought, why don't you explain to me about this void inside and around me, and tell me what to do about it? You would know, you are the person who would know. 'Don't be sad, Louise, you know that *I* love you. Kiss me, Louise, kiss me . . . Would you like us to go to the cinema together?' If that happened, between them they would be able to understand all sorts of things. What things? Oh, don't ask me . . .

Behind Louise's closed eyelids there appeared sketches of two different foreheads: a high, pensive, female one and a plain obstinate one. The two intertwined and became all mixed up – but what does it matter, kiss me, whatever you look like . . .

*

'Odette, get up quick, you're going to be late for school!'

She took the child to school and went on to her work at Madame's house. The day started all over again: she scrubbed, washed, polished the floor, peeled the vegetables. She stayed later today, because there was some ironing to do. At four o'clock Madame said:

'I'm hungry – what about you, Louise?'

She pushed aside the ironing cover and cleared a space on the table. 'Lay the table here in the kitchen, I'll have a little something with you.'

Louise happily did as she suggested.

They sat down opposite each other and Madame helped herself to some jam.

'What about you, Louise, don't you want some jam?'

'No, thank you, I like it better like this.'

Madame spread butter and jam and ate, with her long slender hands. Louise soaked her bread in her coffee and ate slowly, a vague look in her eyes.

It wasn't late and yet already the light coming from the windows was beginning to fade. Summer was slowly dying. Tomorrow it would be autumn, a long succession of days, and after that a whole lifetime to come. An everyday life made up of slow, ordinary days, days without hope. Life would be what it had always had been; but now there would always have been this moment. There would always have been this moment, when Louise was happy with Madame . . . and perhaps before it died Madame might speak.

Leah

Leah

'It's chucking it down,' said the stranger who was standing in front of the open door of the café. The rain splashed on to the pavement and spattered his feet. The air smelled of heat: the day flowed out into the scorching heart of July, and the dark heat in the air seemed as if it had been washed up on earth by the torrential rain. That was how it was raining; that was the kind of storm it had been.

'It's really pelting down,' the stranger said.

'That's obvious,' said the barman. 'Good God, it's obvious enough, there's no need to say it twice.'

It was raining the way it rained in my own part of the country . . . I remembered the day when you and I stood in the corner of a doorway, watching the water streaming down, making rivulets in the ground beneath the apple-trees in the orchard. 'Just look at the water bouncing,' I said, pointing at the stone bench opposite.

' "The water's bouncing" . . . You can see the water bouncing, can you?' you said, smiling.

And we'd started pushing each other out from under the awning, in and out of the rain. After a few minutes of this game, you said, 'You're a crazy girl, really crazy, you're wet through . . .' You brought me back into the corner of the doorway, holding me close. We stayed there like that, your hand on my shoulder, watching the water crushing into the earth the blossom that it had plucked from the apple-trees.

I couldn't see him all the time, the stranger who was watching the rain fall. There was a group standing by the bar and from the table where I was sitting I could see him only when heads and bodies moved, according to the play of the conversations. But I could see the window of the café very clearly – all of it – and behind its backcloth of rain I saw a silhouette sliding past and then, between parted heads, Carrol coming in through the door. Leaning over the bar he said something to the barman, who responded by nodding in my direction. Carrol greeted all the men standing by the bar and ordered a glass of red wine to drink with them. Then, as if he had suddenly spotted me, he walked towards me and stretched out his hand.

'Good evening, Madame,' he said, then returned to his friends. A little while later he came back again and said in a very loud voice, 'Hello again, is everything still OK?'

Sitting down next to me, Carrol leaned across and said in an undertone, 'Leah, I came as soon as I could . . . I had to take the evening tram, those bastards kept us in an hour longer to make us realise they were prepared to force us to buckle under . . . They couldn't have come up with a better trick. As soon as the tram stopped I ran straight here to you; even my mother doesn't know I'm back.'

He was still wearing his factory clothes and his blue canvas jacket was soaked. His thin, bitter face was hardened by anger but his eyes were tender as he looked at me. I watched some fine drops of rain fall from his black hair on to his forehead.

'Leah . . .' he said again.

'You ought to go and change, you're wet through,' I said.

'I want to stay with you.'

'But you might catch cold if you stay soaked like that.'

'I'm boiling with anger,' he said, laughing. 'Don't go away, I'll come back and sit here in a few minutes, I'm just going to finish my drink with the others.'

My eyes wandered over the faces of the workmen, and over Carrol's too. When the heads moved, I could see again the stranger who was standing on the threshold of the café. He was quite alone with the rain, which was falling hard, noisily, on to the cobble-stones of the little street. All of a sudden, the rain seemed to fade away in the reality of the present: it faded even as I watched it, only to switch and become real again, slipping visibly, torrentially, into my memory and furrowing the orchard full of apples. I could hear your voice, I could see your high forehead with its lock of fair hair. We were standing side by side, and the weight of your hand was on my shoulder. We were absolutely the same, not one and the other but one being, and it was like this for an eternity of silence, as if we had come together from the depths of a great abyss of time, and were moving towards the same night, both eaten up by the slow impatience of time.

And so it was every time that we were together. That day when the rain was falling as hard and as noisily as it was now, we went back into the house and closed the door behind us. Sitting at the table, we tucked into our bread without further ado, like children who enjoy themselves while they're eating; and like deprived children at a party we laughed and fought over an apple that was bigger than the others. When we stopped laughing, darkness stretched over our silence. Was it the night that was falling outside and spreading into the room? Was it our night, unfurling in our souls and obscuring everything? I didn't know, I couldn't remember. But I did remember that everything went slowly dark and that in the heart of that darkness my hand met yours. We drew gently closer to each other until our elbows touched.

Everything was upside down. Against my back I could feel the ice cold of a glass of water that had spilled on to the hard wooden table; and there you were leaning on me; and once again we missed our chance of love. And yet, my God, is it not perfection in love when two beings join together in the eternity of a shared night? I felt your freezing hands wander over my body, I felt them grasping my hips and shoulders. Your hands and your eyes, sparkling in the shadow of the terrestrial night and in the shadow of our hearts, were saying, 'You are still alive,' and that 'still' contained a whole future of nothingness, so that 'You are still alive' meant, very precisely, 'You are already dead.'

We went out into the night, our bodies still heavy under their own weight, and walked through the garden, an icy wind lashing our faces and whipping through our clothes. We walked up the road and sat down on the damp earth near some trees halfway up a steep slope. The night was still drenched with rain and the cold froze us to the bone.

You pushed aside some leaves on the earth with your bare hands and arranged some twigs on the place you had cleared. 'The fire won't take,' I said. 'No, it won't,' you replied. You took some matches and paper from your pocket and slipped them under the twigs: for a few moments I could see your pale face in the glow of the flames. We stretched out our hands towards our wet hearth, towards the rising wisp of smoke that was already all that remained of the fire.

'Right, let's warm ourselves up . . .' we said, and we laughed again.

All over the sky black masses were rolling on top of each other and I said, 'Look, they're filling the whole sky, as deep as they are long . . . What's going on? What are they?'

'They're nothing,' you said, 'nothing. They'll continue on their useless course, or else they'll break above our heads, and all we'll get from them is a downpour of icy water.'

I could feel you shudder with cold next to me, and reaching out to touch you I felt the dampness of the garment that was covering your shoulders. The material was cold and soaking wet, as wet as Carrol's jacket had been just now.

I turned back to Carrol. I saw his face, and the way he was looking at me. Seeing that I'd raised my head towards him again, he smiled and handed me a drink.

'Would you like a glass of red wine?'

He placed two glasses on the table and sat down next to me.

'You see, I've come to keep you company.'

We raised our glasses and clinked them. The contact was definitely reassuring. Carrol's glass, compared with his hand, was a small receptacle, quite simple and real; in touching mine it made my glass seem quite simple and real too. But when my glass met *his*, this touching fantasy did not materialise, because the glass which was nothing in my hand met the glass that was nothing in his. What was it that Carrol had just said? 'You see, I've come to keep you company.'

The small café was brightly lit. The men drinking there were letting themselves go a bit after their day's work, talking amongst themselves, and Carrol's face had relaxed slightly. I could see all the shapes and colours clearly, and everything seemed wholly present. Carrol looked at me, then looked around him. The walls were of a faded red colour and covered with a layer of paint which I could touch with my finger and whose precise thickness could be established by flaking off a tiny piece.

'Look,' Carrol said. 'I'll be back in a moment, I must go and reassure my mother and then I'll come back for you here. You'll wait for me, won't you? We'll go to Paulu's together – I've arranged to meet two of my mates there. They're good blokes, you ought to know them. It's us three who've been put in charge of this business at work tomorrow. They're really good mates of mine, we went through the war together, you see, so . . . Anyway, I'll be back in a moment, so you must wait for me here.'

'Yes,' I said. 'You're going to get soaked again, Carrol, it's still raining. Do change your clothes, don't keep that wet jacket on.'

'OK, I'll change,' Carrol said, 'and what's more I'll bring an umbrella for you. Why are you laughing? Isn't it nice of me to bring you an umbrella?'

'Yes, Carrol, it's very nice of you.'

Carrol got up and went out into the alley.

The walls were faded red, the little room was all lit up, and all its colours and shapes seemed vividly present. And yet . . .

I waited for Carrol.

The stranger who was watching the rain left the doorway. Only the big empty doorframe remained, so nothing now obstructed my view. The drops of water were falling more gently, more intermittently. But the stranger hadn't gone altogether; he was still in the alley-way, leaning against the window of the café, still hesitating before going on with his walk. He turned up his collar and slipped his hands into his pockets. I wondered why he didn't come into the café to wait for the rain to stop. Perhaps he had no money, but in a place like this you could come in without any: after you'd stood by the wall for a minute, talking to the people around you, these men would always end up buying you a drink. When you talk together at a bar, you drink together too – that's the way it is. Maybe this man didn't like talking.

Ah, look, there's Jasminot. Jasminot walked past the stranger and came in. He'd just had a shave, and his greying hair was neatly cut: he'd come straight from the barber's. The other men round the bar greeted him with hoots of laughter.

'Hey, Jasminot, don't you look handsome!'

'You in love or something?'

'In love?' Jasminot said. 'It's all very well for you idiots, I'm a lot older than you.'

'Haven't you heard, Jasminot, you're only as old as you feel?'

'Only as old as you feel,' Jasminot said. 'That reminds me of a story I know . . .'

'Come on, tell us, we'll buy you a drink.'

'No, it's my round,' Jasminot said, 'I've only just arrived.'

'Right then, is it a love story?'

'Definitely,' Jasminot said.

'Barman, Jasminot's said he'll stand six drinks . . .'

'Seven including me,' the barman said.

'Once upon a time, there was this poor bloke,' Jasminot said.

'It's not amusing, your story.'

'It's not amusing, but it *is* funny,' Jasminot said.

'We're listening. Thanks, cheers . . .'

'Once upon a time there was this poor bloke,' Jasminot said, 'this poor bloke who had killed his mistress. He'd chopped her up into little pieces and thrown her into the river at nightfall. At the trial, he didn't say anything, he just sat there on his bench looking pathetic, as if he hadn't heard what was going on. "Come on," the judge roared at him, "you must answer the questions. What made you kill your girlfriend?" After a little while the chap opened his mouth and said feebly, "I loved her . . ." The judge yelled, "But for God's sake, man, why did you chop her up into pieces and throw her in the river?" And the chap replied again, "I loved her." "All right," said the judge, "let's leave him be, let's pass sentence and give him hard labour for . . ." '

'For life?'

'No, for twenty years,' Jasminot said, 'but you mustn't interrupt. At the verdict, the bloke still didn't speak; he seemed indifferent, as if he hadn't heard a thing. The judge shouted at him, "Twenty years! Did you hear me? You've got twenty years." The poor bloke lifted his pathetic face a little and said, "When you're in love, you've always got twenty years." '

The men looked at Jasminot as he downed his drink and put his glass back on the counter.

'That's an odd story,' said the barman. 'You've taken us for a ride, Jasminot.'

'It said what it wanted to say,' Jasminot said. 'And that'll

teach you to think I'm a show-off just because I've had my hair
cut.'

Carrol was back. He propped an umbrella up against the bar
and mingled with the group of men.

'You go about with an umbrella these days?' Carouges asked
him.

'And why shouldn't he go about with an umbrella?' Jasminot
said.

Carrol looked at Jasminot and smiled; Jasminot winked back
at him. I couldn't see the man waiting outside the window any
more. He'd gone, I didn't know how long ago – presumably
because the rain had stopped. Yes, Carrol's jacket was perfectly
dry. He'd changed his clothes: he was no longer wearing the
blue canvas jacket, the jacket which had so often been soaked
with rain, cold and wet like the material which my hand had
touched when you and I were sitting on that slope and those
black masses had filled the whole sky above our heads.

You had shivered with cold at my touch and I'd said, 'Let's not
stay here,' but you didn't move. 'You're perished,' I said. 'Let's
go back, or go our separate ways, but let's not stay here.' 'You're
cold too,' you said. We crossed the road and came to the
entrance to the garden, where we paused for a moment in the
silence of the night. And then you said, 'I'm leaving.' You took
my hand and held it in yours, saying, 'You're frozen.' You held
my hand against your cheek, then walked off down the road; I
went back into the house.

I haven't seen you since that night. But there have been long
spells when we haven't met. There was nothing to be done about
it; there was absolutely nothing else to be done. The only way to
construct a life, and to pretend to live, was outside that vision of
ours. But its allure was so strong that in spite of our wish to
escape, whenever we found each other again, by chance or by a
miracle, we were quite unable to part for hours or even days on
end. We stayed close to one another, on the threshold of our
shadowy gate, our hands and bodies totally interlinked in a
fierce tenderness. And if our eyes met, we'd say nothing, but
we'd recognise the very same unique thought that made both
our faces shine. It was as if that vision, which bound us together

quite as strongly as the force which made us reject each other, was our only possible hope, our only chance of salvation.

'Shall we go to Paulu's place, then?' Carrol said.

'Yes,' I said.

It was dark in the alley, but it was no longer raining, so Carrol's umbrella had become unnecessary. He used it like a walking stick – it was the only sound that accompanied us on our way. As we crossed the little square, a swirl of wind shook the trees, releasing a brief shower of uneven raindrops. Suddenly, the view opened up and I could see, in the distance, that the sky had cleared; I could already see the glimmer of a clear night on the mountains. But still rising from the ground was that beautiful after-storm smell, a perfume hot and wet at the same time; it was as if the heat in the air was finally releasing itself after flowing back into the earth under the torrential rain. Everywhere there was silence and torpor: on the vines and the hard agaves, in the undergrowth, everywhere.

'We can go straight in, there's no doorbell or knocker.'

Carrol was speaking. I didn't realise that we'd arrived at Paulu's house. I thought I was alone, and that the road had no end.

The square of paved ground in front of the house was all shadows. The door opened directly into the kitchen.

'Is Paulu in?' Carrol asked.

'He's not back yet,' Paulu's wife said, 'but your mates are already here.'

Carrol walked through into the room next to the kitchen. I decided to stay with Paulu's wife for a moment. She was folding some sheets and piling them into a basket.

'Let me help you,' I said.

'Don't bother, it's not worth it,' she said. 'D'you know, I'm really worried about these schemes they're cooking up. If only they could have at least all acted together . . .'

'But they've been trying to get to that position for a month now,' I said. 'They had no option but to act on their own.'

'The truth is . . .' she said.

'Come on!' Carrol shouted. 'Aren't you going to come and say hello?'

I went into the next room and shook hands with Carrol's friends.

'This is Leslie Fay, and this is Gab Ortiguez,' Carrol said.

'Have you finished working out your plans?' I asked, for something to say.

'We're only just beginning,' Leslie said, looking at me with his small laughing eyes. 'Once, you see, we three got together to defend something or other to do with liberty, with the beauty of the world – but right now we've met to defend our beefsteak.'

'The country stinks,' Carrol said.

'Oh, give over,' Ortiguez said. 'You and your fine phrases and your formulas.'

These two lads weren't at all like Carrol and I wondered what they were up to in his factory. Leslie Fay spoke with an accent that came from a long way away – not to mention his name. Fay, Ortiguez and Carrol were of an age, barely over twenty, and all three wore the enamel parachutists' badge on their jacket lapels. Otherwise these two lads weren't at all like Carrol. Everything about them – their attitudes, their gestures, their voices – showed that they had something to avenge, probably an adolescence that had been cut to shreds by barbed-wire entanglements, sucked in through successive layers of atmosphere at the heart of those heavy nights when they made their strange visitations from sky to earth. They had lost everything and they knew it, and this was at once their strength and their misfortune.

Carrol had lost everything too, but he didn't know it, and this was both his weakness and his good luck. One day, in the depths of a wood where the trees had been ripped apart, they had needed his simplicity, and this need had become rooted in them. But the friendship linking all three – an invulnerable friendship, born at the bottom of a hole of mud and solitude – was dangerous for little Carrol.

Standing by the window, Carrol said, 'I think I can hear Paulu coming.'

'Good, I'll leave you to your discussion,' I said.

'You want to leave?' Carrol said softly. 'Why do you want to leave? I don't like you leaving me like this. I'll come by this evening.'

*

It was dark outside. I resumed my walk up the road and into the night – because the night restored to me your presence. It reunited us, you and me, but it also gave me you on your own, outside of me, exactly as you really were, your tall, skinny figure all eaten up with nerves, ready to engage with trouble whenever you saw it arising anywhere in the world.

The night was all around me, and you were in the night by my side. I could see you in the streets of strife-torn Shanghai, in that inadequately armoured lorry; in Belgium, in a tank stuck in a muddy ditch, lying flat against the jammed door, listening for the deadly sound of the shell and regretting that you would not meet your death under a sky full of stars. I saw you near a snow-covered rock on that turning on the road to Navacerrada, the butt of your rifle squeezed between your heels, crouched in the undergrowth next to your chief, an old gypsy type of seventy; I saw you in a mauve twilight on the coast of Somalia. You were always yourself, exactly the same, never mind what part of the world you'd come back from, skinnier, nervier than ever.

'Well?' I asked you.

'Nothing,' you replied.

You smiled at me, with that smile that's diabolical and resigned at the same time; you smiled at me with your whole face, and then you began to talk, and your lips and teeth moved rapidly to keep up with the words that slipped and flowed out of your mouth. You spoke of Shanghai and Madrid, of the fighting in Beauce and in Burma; you spoke of a whole procession of people, of dangerous situations and countries, and how you mingled with them and drew them back into yourself, not so as to feel at one with the world but so as to tear yourself away from it. 'Out of all that, the only thing I possess is . . .'

I could hear your voice telling me that, in the presence of the royal head of black stone that you brought back to Europe: it had a death warrant inscribed on it. I was in the night that restored you to me, I was completely enveloped in a night that was more than the night which covered the trees, the stones, the animals beneath the leaves; it was a night in which you and I were together, not as one and the other but as a single being, both equally worn down by the slow impatience of time.

Retracing my steps I arrived back at Paulu's house, where I

could see, in the square of light cast by the window, Carrol, Paulu, Leslie and Ortiguez sitting round the table. I walked softly, taking care not to stumble over the stones in the road. They didn't hear me go past, and I walked on faster, until I got to Jasminot's house.

I found him sitting in the kitchen with a shoe-last between his knees, repairing the shoes of his youngest child; his wife and children were in bed. He was leaning forward intently as he nailed, smoothed and polished the shoe of a four-year-old, all worn down at the toe. He looked up as I came in and said:

'Hello, Leah, I'm glad you've dropped in. There's something bothering you, isn't there?'

'Yes,' I said.

'Tomorrow we'll go there together,' Jasminot said, 'we'll both go over there early.'

'Do you think they'll succeed in doing anything?'

'They're kids. There's fifty of them, that makes five pickets of ten, and there are two thousand workers. On top of that their boss is an arsehole.'

'And there's nothing we can do to help them? Nothing at all?'

'What could we do?' said Jasminot. 'We're nothing, we're less than nothing.'

I didn't speak, as if put in my place, the only place I deserved. At regular intervals Jasminot tapped, with a sharp blow, on each nail that he had already half-inserted with his finger.

'The number,' Jasminot said. 'The number, and the time.'

He said these two words in a strange way, as if he was putting them in capital letters, or investing them with a sense of black magic. He went on:

'One part evil is always much more powerful than one part good. Evil has a habit of leaking, spreading out, overlapping, before you know where you are – that's just the way it is. You need at least a thousand good men to triumph over one evil one.'

'Even so,' I said, 'it's sometimes happened that a small number of people have . . .'

'No, it hasn't,' Jasminot said. 'That's never happened. Oh, all right, maybe it is possible for one good part to triumph over an evil part of equal size, or bigger even, but only given time, given a great deal of time. You might almost say, given an eternity.'

Jasminot's last words, which he said softly, tenderly almost, seemed to have had a calming effect on him. Now he was quiet. Slowly he filed the leather on the edge of the shoe, so as to give the sole its proper shape. Lifting the shoe off the last he placed it on the table, where it stood quite straight, the end slightly raised up like the prow of a ship, in good shape on its bright new sole.

'Shall we talk about the other thing now?' I said.

'No, let's leave the other thing till tomorrow,' Jasminot said. 'Now we're going to eat something really good.'

He put a kind of tart on the table and we helped ourselves to slices of golden pastry topped with olives and anchovies. Jasminot ate slowly, with an expression on his face that was composed but not happy.

We made arrangements to leave very early in the morning. I shook his hand and had already begun to walk up the road when he called out to me: 'Leah! Be affectionate with Carrol.'

'I am,' I said. 'As much as I possibly can be.'

It was a calm night and the stars – those same stars which you'd regretted not being able to see when you thought you were about to die – were shining brightly. It had got warmer, and a light wind had nearly dried the cobble-stones; only a few puddles of water still remained, in places where the ground was uneven. When I arrived at my house Carrol was already there, sitting on the window-sill.

'The door's not locked,' I said, 'why didn't you go in?'

'I don't dare go in when you're not there,' Carrol said. 'I'm always afraid Germinie will still be in her kitchen.'

We crossed Germinie's kitchen in the dark. I switched on the light in my bedroom and Carrol pulled me close. I put my hand on his head, gently stroking his black hair.

'You are my wife . . .' Carrol said. 'It's true, isn't it, you're my wife?'

'The night,' I said, 'look at the night.'

'What do you mean, what night?' Carrol said as I dragged him to the window.

Carrol took me in his arms again and I went on stroking his hair. He leaned his head on my shoulder and talked, but I couldn't hear what he was saying; I was talking too, and staring out into the darkness.

'Leah,' Carrol said, 'Leah, what are you talking about?'

Shutting the window I held him close for a long moment, then led him back through Germinie's dark kitchen.

'What time will you be leaving?' I asked.

'Now,' Carrol said. 'I am leaving now, on Ortiguez's motorbike.'

I turned out the light in my bedroom and opened the window.

It was the next day. Although early morning, heat was already in the air and the sky was very clear, yesterday's storm having swept away the clouds. Jasminot and I got on the bus together but barely spoke the whole length of the journey. As we drove down from the mountains and towards the town, the heat became overwhelming. There was a slight breeze in the vehicle, which refreshed us a bit, but once we got off the bus in town it was like walking into a furnace: there wasn't a breath of air. And then we came to the southern entrance of the factory, a great mass of red brick. The gates were closed and the approach road strangely was calm, an outside calm surrounding the hum of the usual morning activity. I looked at Jasminot, and Jasminot looked at me.

'Doesn't look as if they made it,' he said.

We walked around the factory but only encountered two or three women with shopping bags. At the northern entrance there was the same atmosphere of calm surrounding the usual morning activity. The sun heated the space, burning every brick of the building and every stone of the pavement. On the road, a square of asphalt, blacker than the rest of the earth, seemed to be slowly remelting, giving off a heavy smell. We walked aimlessly, in this burning void, in this desert of stones, along these dumb bricks that enclosed the usual murmur, separating us from it, rejecting us, forbidding us. I was hot, I had never been so hot in my whole life. I leant against the brick wall.

'Jasminot . . .' I said.

I had shouted, rather than spoken, his name. Jasminot took me by the shoulders and shook me gently. 'Pull yourself together, Leah . . .'

We crossed the road into a sort of wide forecourt in front of the factory, then wandered down a tree-lined pavement. We looked instinctively inside each café, but they were all completely quiet.

'Look over there,' I said. 'Look, I can see a motorbike near the pavement of a little café. Carrol came here on Ortiguez's motorbike . . .'

I dragged him over to it.

'There's more than one motorbike in town,' Jasminot said.

But I had noticed, tied to the saddle, the light blue pullover that Carrol took with him in the cool night hours.

We found Ortiguez in the café.

'Where's Carrol?' I asked. 'And what's been going on?'

'Carrol's fine,' Ortiguez said. 'Only a little graze on the hand; a scratch, you might call it. Otherwise . . .'

Jasminot and I waited for him to continue. We had been floundering in the empty heat, and our faces must have been sweaty, bewildered, desperate for the slightest bit of information. Ortiguez looked at us and started to laugh; we went on waiting.

'Don't laugh at us like that,' Jasminot said.

'Otherwise,' Ortiguez said, 'it lasted for less than a quarter of an hour. We found that there were eight of us. A picket of eight,' and he started laughing again.

'What about the forty-two others?' I said.

Ortiguez stopped laughing and looked straight in front of him, his face seized with a terrible indifference. Out of the silence which had just been created, and without changing his expression, he said, 'They turned up along with all the others, at the usual time, with their packets under their arms. They'd been bought off – Grozzi bought them off, yesterday evening.'

'It's even shittier than I thought,' said Jasminot.

'Who's Grozzi?' I said.

'You must know him,' Jasminot said. 'He's that skinny chap with black hair, just now he's living on the road leading up to the old fort, past our village.'

'Go on,' I said, 'I understand less and less about this business . . .'

'In fact, it's dead simple,' Ortiguez said.

'Go on,' Jasminot said too.

'So then,' Ortiguez said, 'smarting under the new shock of having been shamefully abandoned, we started to wave our hands about a bit – eight of us against two thousand minus eight. There were two or three punches and a lot of jeering; you couldn't move. Paulu threw himself on to Fat Charles, the fellow we'd really counted on, and straight away three guys held Paulu back, but Paulu kept on shouting: "You've been paid off then, have you, you bastard? You've been paid off, have you?" "So what?" said Fat Charles. "It's better to be paid off than to be out of work." Another guy said, "You had no reason to go against the crowd when even the union hadn't agreed." And then lots of things along the lines of "We're fed up with strikes, we've been at it for two years without achieving anything . . ." No, it lasted less than a quarter of an hour, then the work siren sounded and everyone was dragged along by the flood of people going in.'

'What about Carrol?' I said. 'Did he go back to work, just like that?'

'What else do you expect him to do?' Jasminot said.

'But what about you?' I said to Ortiguez.

'Oh, I don't need the money,' he said.

'You have money?' Jasminot asked.

'I've got that much,' Ortiguez said, pulling two crumpled hundred-franc notes out of his pocket. 'That's what I've got, but I really don't give a damn.'

'And you came straight here?' Jasminot asked.

'It's been two hours since the stupid business was over, and I've had time to find out about a few things. I know people in this town.'

'The fellows around here know what to expect when he's involved,' Jasminot said. 'Whenever something fishy happens Grozzi's behind it. Everyone loathes him. But people round here are capable of letting themselves be exterminated like rats.'

'There's more to it yet,' Ortiguez said. 'One of the directors came and harangued us, just the eight of us. He went on about "the untimeliness of a reassessment of salaries". *In view*, he said, of the fact that increases in taxes at the production stage would hardly affect retail prices at the consumer stage, and *in view* of the fact that it would therefore be unfair for the owners to have to bear the burden imposed by the new tax all alone. *Moreover*, he said, there was now a chance to reduce the hours of work, and consequently the rate of pay. I didn't wait for the end of the lecture, I picked up my cap and walked out. I'm quite prepared to lose everything and to be on the losing side but I don't like the idea of being made a fool of.'

'What about Leslie?' I said.

'Leslie stayed behind. He can always push off, back to England, to Mama and Papa and Cambridge and all that. Maybe he didn't like the thought of leaving Carrol.'

Ortiguez had produced a small stick, I don't know where it came from, which he began to slash with his pen-knife. He went on doing this for several minutes, then he put the piece of wood on the table, next to his crumpled fortune. And once again his indifferent eyes looked straight ahead.

'That was a lousy business,' Ortiguez said. 'I really don't give a damn.'

'Who's Grozzi?' I said.

'I told you,' Jasminot replied, 'he's that tall, thin, dark-skinned guy; some say he's Spanish, others Italian. Every now and again he comes and stays here for a month or two, and he seems to get by in some way, making money out of the land round here. At the moment he's running a smallholding by himself on the road to the old fort. As soon as he turns up, people say that everything starts to go wrong. It might be a bad crop, or a girl leaving a man, or a kid catching fever – people always say, "It's Grozzi's fault." When things come out in the open, like they did this morning, he'll go away for a bit, he'll go back to his own country. It's a wonder how he manages to get across the border all the time so easily. I tell you, tomorrow or the next day, he won't be around in the village any more, you won't see him until enough time has passed for people to forget it. He'd do better to stay there, wherever it is he lives across the border.'

'Isn't it possible to get a chap like that arrested?' I said.

'By whom and for what?' Ortiguez said. 'My dear lady, you make it sound all too easy.'

Ortiguez began to laugh, very softly, and then he went quiet. For some time we sat there leaning on the table, all three of us, dumb, immobile.

'Who's Grozzi?' I said.

'For God's sake, Leah!' Jasminot said.

I was overcome with the heat again, just as I had been earlier in front of the silent factory: it was as if the sun was pouring on to my skin and coating it.

'We might as well go back,' Jasminot said. 'Let's go back to the village, I've got work to do.'

'I'll come back up this evening with Carrol and Leslie,' Ortiguez said.

As we were leaving the café Jasminot said, 'Are you coming back with me?'

'No,' I said, 'I'm going to walk for a bit. I'll see you again this evening.'

I shook Jasminot's hand and walked down the road. I walked without knowing where I was going, among a great mass of walls and burning paving-stones, a display of blues, yellows and tortured reds, like a burst of blood in the heat. In my anguish at this flashing and fusion of colour and heat, which seemed to spread all over the town, I walked as if I was wounded: at the heart of my anguish lay a single question, which seemed almost to be dictated by the colours and the heat themselves. Its rhythmical formula nagged at me continually: 'Who's Grozzi?'

I walked through the horror of that hot, bright town, a fanfare of sunlight in which peeping insects with tiny feet and lemon-coloured wings settled between the paving-stones and on the burning walls. These insects were brittle, dry, bright and noisy. They had long red and yellow bodies with long thin feet and wings, and the bulging eyes of daytime voyeurs. At night the only thing that distinguished them from the faded dark was the glossy black of their beautiful gleaming shells.

I went on walking, still wounded by all the luminous blues and yellows, but all of a sudden the nagging question stopped, leaving nothing for my aching eyes to gaze on but the hideous heat and colours, now silent, as if in deliberate response to the new quietness around them. In a strange calm, as if there was nothing left of my repulsion but a kind of fatigue, I sat down on a low wall surrounding a square. Yes, I said to myself, there were people who crossed frontiers by underground passages, risking their lives as they wormed their way through mud and rubble, their clothes always covered with clay, their faces darkened by all the shadows of the earth; and there were people who crossed frontiers under an open sky, their clothes always clean and, as the saying goes, spick and span.

I'd been talking to myself, in an undertone. A child stopped in front of me, a loaf of bread under his arm, and looked at me curiously. I stopped talking to myself and smiled at him, just like a normal person. He went off, disappointed, then came back for a moment, with the look on his face of a child who's been swindled.

That's how Carrol would be looking now, I thought, as he leaned over his machine. I thought back over the events of yesterday and of this morning, I thought about all the things that had brought me to this torrid town. They were little things, really, they didn't mean very much if you took them at face value. But if you looked beyond that . . . 'The number and the time,' Jasminot had said. That was all very well, but when there was only one of you, and you were worn down by the slow impatience of time . . .

I looked round me again, at the wounding colours and the silent heat. Everything was quiet, and I was still calm. I walked a little further around the town and made my way to the station and the bus terminal. Once on the bus I picked a seat near an open window, but it didn't take the bus long to get out of the hot streets; I could soon glimpse sea beyond the tree-covered slopes. But then the bus took a route inland, away from the coast. We were going to drive up to the hills, and then to the mountains. By then I was no longer concerned about the passing of time, I had stopped looking out of the window. A cool breeze wafted over my still sweaty face and I felt almost cold. I lowered my eyelids and entered into the presence of darkness.

I got off the bus at the edge of the village and instead of walking into the centre, I headed off towards a vast clump of bamboo, where I'd left my bike yesterday before the storm. I'd wanted to follow the long path that winds up the mountain to where the view stretches all the way to the sea, but as soon as I had reached the top the first drops of rain began to fall, and I'd walked back down via a short cut which led to the heart of the village.

My bike was just where I'd left it the day before. I pulled it out from among the branches and rode off at full speed, so as to put as much distance as possible between me and the village. Before long the steepness of the hill meant that I had to slow down, or get off and push. When the road finally ceased to climb, I was a good five kilometres from the village, and it completely vanished behind me as I began to go downhill. I could already see a second hill ahead, which would mean another climb. Just before embarking on it I stopped in the valley for a moment, a false, blind valley where nothing grew but dried-up plants among yellow rocks. Behind me rose the silent hill. From this side there was nothing to give any indication that there was a village clinging to the other slope.

In front of me, at the very top of the next hill, I could see the brownish mass of the old fort. On the slope leading to it, much closer, stood the house. In the midst of all that aridity, the few standing vines and the surrounding olive trees made it seem like an oasis.

Looking around me, I took in the whole amphitheatre of dry hills. There was no fresh air here at all, and at this time of day the heat was still strong; my whole body was again soaked with sweat. On the ground the dry-skinned insects were making a deafening racket. It was sunset: the sun was no longer visible on the restricted horizon, but it had left its bloody trails in the sky. I formed such a clear impression in my mind of the lie of the land in front of me that I could have found my way around it blindfolded. But now I had to leave to start on my return journey. I climbed the silent side of the hill, and then as I made my way down the winding road the village slowly began to reappear before my eyes.

When I reached the clump of bamboo, I put my bike back under the branches.

I dropped in very briefly at my own place and, hurrying now, I made for the heart of the village.

Yes, I was in a hurry now. I was in a hurry to move on, and to have my say.

Jasminot, Carrol, Leslie and Ortiguez were all in the small café, standing by the bar with a group of people. As I shook hands with them, I saw Carrol's eyes linger tenderly on the little jacket I'd thrown over my shoulders at home. It's true, it was a smart jacket and one I didn't often wear, but I hadn't put it on because of that.

Carrol came up to me and lightly touched my wrist in a sad caress. 'Lea, my love,' he said. I drank the wine that my comrades gave me; but when I held out my hand to take the glass, and raised it to Carrol's, it was as if it had really remained inert on the bar, as if it was waiting for something. The curve traced by my hand as it rose with the glass reminded me of the

dots that children have to join up into a line with a black pen in
drawing books. The raised hand signified nothing at all; no
movement counted, the only truth was that my hand had really
remained inert on the bar, waiting for something, so that it was
the invisible hand that drew the firm black outlines.

Jasminot was talking to me, everyone was talking to me, but I
didn't hear them. I answered them but I didn't hear my
answers. At that moment their words had absolutely no
importance for me. All I was waiting for was nightfall, for the
day to be well and truly over, as the shouting of a crowd dies
away.

As I slipped on my jacket Carrol started playing with my belt,
laying it flat on the bar, wrapping it round his wrist. 'Give it
here,' I said. I tied the belt firmly round my waist and bade the
men farewell.

It was already good and dark outside, though errant patches of
light still penetrated the blackness from time to time. I walked
slowly towards the clump of bamboo, as if I were out for a stroll,
and, just like before, I soon found my bike under the branches,
then made my way up and down the same slopes. Beyond the
hills, in the depths of the night, some rosy tints still lingered,
looking as if they were about to fade into nothing. I don't know
whether my journey lasted two hours or a few minutes – I had
absolutely no sense of the weight of time.

I crossed the narrow, blind rocky valley, now completely
dark, feeling the dried-up plants beneath my feet, and lay my
bike down under the first olive tree I reached. A dim light came
from each of the windows to the left and right of the door. I made
no noise – I had on the cord espadrilles worn by all the people
round here and I was able to walk softly up to the house. Pressing
my face against the window, I looked through the canvas
curtains into the room and saw a man lying fully dressed on a
narrow bed. He had a thin face and black hair, and there was
something rather appealing about his features. 'Some people
said he was a big black Spaniard, others said he was Italian . . .'
There was neither ugliness nor evil in his face – more a profane
obliviousness.

A half-full suitcase lay open on the table and there was an
alarm clock by the side of the bed, as if the man was resting

before a dawn start. I closed my eyes for a moment. What if I continued my journey, I thought, what if I went on climbing the hills beyond? The time would surely come when I would rest by the side of the road and this man would pass me. He'd be at the start of a journey, with a fresh early-morning taste on his lips, and the first rays of the sun would shine on my forehead and impregnate my heart.

I was standing right next to the door – if I tried the latch in the hope that it would yield, it might make a noise. I looked into the house again and saw a half-open door in the partition at the far end of the room, very near the bed. I went round the house, sticking close to the walls, feeling my way along them with my hands. The back room was completely dark apart from a crack of light from the half-open door that connected it to the front room, and one of the windows was open. Pushing gently against the unlit pane I climbed through and walked silently into the room. I stopped for a moment in front of the half-open door, on the threshhold of the front room, and I took from my jacket pocket the little Corsican knife that you gave me. I walked into the light.

I shouted, 'Grozzi!' He opened his eyes and saw me through the mist of a too sudden awakening. He half sat up to grab my arm but before he could do so, I had my arm around his shoulders as if to embrace him; my hand was against his back, and I struck him. He started and fell back on my arm, crushing it. I tried to pull it out from beneath his back. He grabbed me by the shoulders to push me away but the sharp pain in his back prevented him from straightening up, from pushing me away. For a moment we stayed like this, him lying flat with his arms outstretched, his hands pushing against my shoulders, and me resisting this pressure with all the strength in my body.

At last I freed my arm. I thrust it towards him and struck him again and again right in the middle of his torso, I don't know how many times, until blood began to stain the linen and my hands, until the arms which were grasping my shoulders fell back across my body, and his head moved slowly from side to side, several times. Three or four times, at long intervals, I was assailed by deep breaths from his big open mouth. Finally he was still, and I was confronted by its abyss. As I closed his jaw with my hands there rose in me an overwhelming grief, heavy with poisonous dregs. I sat there for a long time, my hands pressed against his face, while my heart slowed down and my hands became accustomed to the stillness and coldness of death. That is how it all happened; and it happened yesterday, in the night.

I left the house for a moment. Darkness surrounded me, and I felt very calm, but I would have liked it to have been raining. I searched all the corners and sheds in the garden and found a wide shovel with a long handle which I propped up on my bike, tying it to the handlebars and the saddle. Then I went back in and stood close to him. His face was already calm and beautiful. I folded the blanket he'd slept on around him twice, and covered his body with all the bitter passion I still felt for the colour of blood. I brought my bike in and by leaning it against the bed I managed to slide the body on to the iron part of the shovel, securing it firmly to the saddle with my belt. This is how I managed to take the body through the scrub and undergrowth of the region to a wood of holly oaks, where the perpetual shade offered by the trees made the ground softer. It must have been after, but not much after, midnight; it could have been either the first or the last hour of the day.

I dug deep, for hours on end. Although the ground was less dry here, the effort was more than a woman's arms could manage. I did it, though, and then I laid him at the bottom of my pit. Before throwing the heaped up earth back on to him, I put one of my own handkerchiefs on his face, on the face of the man who for me had no name.

Then I left the oak wood and came back through the scrub, to the heart of endless solitude. The lights were still on in the house. I tidied up the room and, finding linen and various other things inside a wardrobe, threw them in the suitcases – except for two items of identification, which I held on to: some kind of pass written in Spanish, in the name of Ferralle, and an alien's identity card, issued in France, in the name of Luiggi. He must have kept the papers that were in the name of Grozzi in a wallet in the clothes that he'd been wearing. I slipped the suitcase under the wardrobe and put the shovel back in the shed where I'd found it. At last I set off along the merciless road. Before broaching the last climb, I threw the identity cards into a heap on the wayside and set fire to them. I watched the flames spread to the plants nearby.

I didn't stop again before reaching the bamboo where I left my bike and returned to the village at an easy pace. I saw the top of the hill glowing red: some bushes must have caught for it to have reached that far. There was nothing unusual about a fire in this part of the world. For me, this fire at the edge of the night was all that my eyes could bear; already today's dawn was rising on the village, whilst all that was spreading over me was the death of my cruel day and my pity for his blood.

Carrol turned up this evening. 'How cold your hands are,' he said. They were white and bloodless. I tried to raise them to touch his black hair but they fell back at my side, inert. After I had led Carrol back across Germinie's dark kitchen, I began to write all this down.

I've only wanted to retrace my movements, not really my thoughts: I haven't spoken of my own grief. I've only spoken of the colours that wounded my eyes, of the tiredness of my arms and the pallor of my hands. Do you need any more to understand what I did?

Here is the dawn again. There's no doubt that we are in for a season of storms: yet another one has hit the village. The water will wash away any trace of blood that might have marked the stones and the earth up on the hills. But I'm writing this under cover: I won't let any water dilute the ink with which I'm recording my story for you. My killing, my rupture, will live on inside me for ever.

Let it rain, dear God, let it rain again on my cold country . . . Let a torrential rain wash away all colour and all life. When will that time come when we shall be once more at each other's side, on the threshold of the shadowy gate where all daylight's games are shattered for ever?

Clara

Clara

Her hair was arranged in two criss-crossing plaits on top of her bent head, and her hands, lying in the lap of her dress, were very pale; she had become altogether lighter, transparent almost. She was so fair, so slender and so light, and now she had been released from the weight of the world. In silence. When a tram or heavy lorry passed in the street her body knew of it only by the slightest of contacts, by a subtle shuddering of the floor beneath her feet. Silence. Her lowered eyelids insulated her from colours and from shapes: she had already slipped into a world that had no limits. She was almost in a state of bliss.

That is how my Lennie's image comes back to me, and it's at that point in the past that I recall the glow of her words – after those two days of paralysis that were merely a pontoon bridge between life and death. I wish our eyes could meet again as they used to. I wish our silent words could bind us together on that slippery ice that is the purity of her death.

'We're not going any further – what about you, Clara, are you coming back with us?'

'No, I'll go all the way.'

I wanted no more of their whispered voices. I wanted the dark drapes to be torn off and thrown away: I wanted her to be covered with all those flowers and to be freed from all the heaviness, all the tears. I wanted her to be given back her piece of the sky and of the earth.

Slowly my steps caught up with the others following her. Yes, that was my Lennie, sitting down, hair in criss-crossed plaits on her bent head, pale hands in the lap of her dress, halfway to slipping into a universe without limits. Almost in a state of bliss.

It was the second time. She had tried to reject her life once before, but the blood that flowed from her open wrists had been staunched, and washed out of her dress. The poisoned spring had never been purged. How quickly the sight of blood frightens people! Did they think that to see her life restored would stop her thinking of death? This time Lennie made sure she would succeed. Instead of calling out to death or letting it creep gently into her, susceptible to time or help, she threw herself right into the very heart of it, like a bird that wants to take flight, swooping into the sky from the top storey of a building, or like a flower thrown from a window at a passing conqueror.

A woman had come into the bedroom and Lennie had seen her lips move. The woman spoke but Lennie didn't answer. Bending over her, she projected sounds and words into Lennie's ear. These noises and words hurt me so much, Lennie thought, why do people distress me like this? 'No,' she said. Smiling, the woman asked her whether she was cold, whether she'd like something to eat or drink. Lennie said what was needed and the woman left. Lennie looked round the room, now freed from anyone's presence, and fixed her eyes on the high, difficult window. It was the only thing that mattered to her.

She could see the night against the window-panes. No, she thought, not in the night; in the morning, so that she'd be facing the light, as if facing hope. The window was high and difficult and it was the only thing that mattered. Lennie lowered her eyelids. Someone opened the door: she could feel the draught of cold air on her arms and legs. Who's bothering me now? Turning her head she opened her eyes and in front of the half-open door stood her child, all clean in his flowered pyjamas. He was moving his lips.

'Come on in, then,' Lennie said. The child's lips were moving: he was waiting for Lennie to move towards the jewel case on the table, for her to take out an object shaped like a horn and place it against one side of her face. The child was waiting for the large black shell that would let him be heard by his mother.

Lennie's hand didn't move. 'Off you go, then,' she said. She was alone again, she was light and she was free, and her hands were lying in the lap of her dress.

'How my death embarrasses you, Clara . . . No, my hand didn't move, I didn't hold this strange black shell up to my face. My vastness is without waves and without submarine fauna and no shell carries its echoes into it, no mother-of-pearl can transmit its murmurs. What did my child have to do with my movements of death?

'I could tell when it was you they were talking about, Clara, because the harsh, clamorous sound of your name came through to me. You loved me – but now you rend my heart, as if you were crying out instead of speaking to me: your name rends me like a cry.

(The woman came in. 'Aren't you hungry, aren't you cold?' 'No,' Lennie said.)

'It's not very long since we met. I was sitting with a group of happy, pretty women, and some men who were talking to each other. You were sitting opposite, watching me: sometimes someone spoke to you . . . Your name rends me like a cry. As I held the black shell up to my face your look distressed me and I put the strange object back in its case. You smiled at me, Clara, and I smiled back. You knew the price of my silence – you knew that locked in my silence I could wander in all kinds of unknown sounds, just as the seeker of buried treasure is attentive to the signs wherever he goes. And because of this you believe that I died not so much because of my silence, but rather thanks to it. And yet my death still embarrasses you . . .

'Another day, you lit a fire when I was in the room with you. You picked up some logs, and your hands lingered over the pattern of the wood, as if the marks had some meaning, and they lingered too over the particles of soil and the moss that was still sticking to the bark. White flakes fell off the moss into your hands; you could see right through them, tiny whitish specks. We didn't say anything, but you put the white flakes back under the moss, and I put the log on a piece of furniture behind me. Through this infinitesimal fragment, the forest haunted us still. We didn't say anything but we turned the mystery over in our minds, and our hands were a part of the miracle. We had to remain silent, and let everything fall apart.

'Someone came into the room then, and we talked and drank our tea with proper decorum. How calmly one behaves in the face of anguish, mysteries and miracles. I no longer wanted to put up with that kind of proper behaviour, nothing had any value except as a symbol or a word, and I could no longer build on that. I needed my truth, Clara. I wanted to rejoin the great

gulf of infinite truth, where everything is pure beginning; I
wanted to be part of the eternally recurring event again. Freed
from all other passion, the only thing that was pushing me
towards death was death itself: I didn't call for it as one cries for
help, but I threw myself at the heart of death . . . I was free and
that is what I chose to do. Will you tell me that it wasn't a choice
but a refusal? Clara, is a choice ever anything but a refusal? I
needed my truth, I needed my death as I needed eternity . . .'

'She was deaf. It seems it's worse than being blind.'
    'It's right at the end there, in the fifth avenue. Are you cold,
Clara?'
    'No, I'm not cold.'
    And keep your peace, while we're following her dead body.
Footsteps and footsteps, my steps in yours – but leave me be,
leave me to walk by myself. Lennie: light, transparent, hair in
criss-crossing plaits on top of her bent head. 'Off you go, then,'
Lennie had said to her child. She was alone again now,
immobile, free.
    'No, my hand didn't move. Did you expect me to cry out,
then, to let these child's arms join round my neck to make a link
which would restrain me? Did you see the flowered pyjamas that
the child wore in readiness for his innocent night as a symbol of
humanity? No, my kingdom has no symbols and no legends.
That's not where the crowd is, the heart of the crowd.
    'My source is pure, nothing needs interpretation. I was in
silence, Clara, and thus almost in God. My sea had no black
shell, and the sweetness of my death will be transmitted to you in
spite of logic. And then it will no longer be a dialogue.'

A sun without warmth touched the half-open earth. There was
no rustling in the trees bordering the avenues, no sign in the
colour of the air. Neither joy nor pain destroyed space or time,
and nothing moved in the watching universe: it was not
transient. No fragment of space or of time slipped in with Lennie
when, light and transparent, she slid from four men's arms
without weighting down the earth. All around her there was a
startled sweetness.
    The sweetness was there again in five more avenues – and
then there was a road: long, calm and indifferent. More

footsteps, and my steps in these other steps. It was indeed not logical that Lennie's death should have been transmitted to me ... all is pure refusal in the watching world. It is not transient: if one doesn't preserve in oneself a fragment of space or of time, then ...

'Are we all getting the bus?'

'Yes, come to my place; I'll make some tea, that'll warm us up.'

'Clara, will you come too? I know you're cold; it's true, isn't it, you're cold?'

'No, I'm not cold.'

From you to me, bound together in silence. You opened the window on the rising dawn, the silent dawn which brought with it a song of endless shadows. At last everything was going to be born, and the time for words would come. Oh Lennie, from what pride, what weakness, what fascination, did you ... Did you think that you had only to die to slip into the heart of the universe? The lips of the child moved, and your hand remained still!

Now the road was empty of any faces that she knew. Clara walked on slowly, without companions, through an unfamiliar burble of words and sounds. A cart passed by, some children shrieked, she could see countryside on both sides. In the village square she got on to an empty bus. As he waited for his passengers, the driver jumped up and down to warm himself and blew hot breath into his gloves. A man got on the bus and as he passed the driver he slapped him on the shoulder in a friendly gesture.

'You going into town?' the driver asked.

'Yes, I thought I'd go to the cinema,' said the man.

A couple came next. The woman said, 'We're going to pick up a sack of wood.'

The driver, who was issuing the tickets himself, stretched across Clara towards the half-open window. 'Would you like me to shut it, are you cold?' he asked her.

'Yes,' she said.

Silence. The driver closed the window, sat down and started up the bus. Black branches of passing trees brushed against the windows, and fields stretched out beyond them. Darkness fell, and in the distance clouds banked and turned red, as though the night was sacred. 'Yes, we're going to pick up some wood,' the woman said. She opened a paper bag and handed her boyfriend a sweet – purple, shaped like a violet.

Blanche

Blanche

'Blanche, is my shirt ironed?'

No answer. He shouted down again: 'Blanche!'

He was on the landing, stripped to the waist. Blanche hadn't heard him. It wasn't worth shouting again: he knew she wouldn't have ironed his shirt. He went back into the bedroom. Too bad, he could put on the one he had worn the day before. Blanche was an absent-minded woman and she often forgot things that he had asked her to do. He'd have liked to put on a clean shirt, though. It was a bore, Blanche being so absent-minded. In three minutes he was dressed: tie knotted, hair combed. He went downstairs and collected his hat and overcoat. As he passed the kitchen door he could see Blanche standing there, her hand outstretched towards the cupboard, as if she was just about to open it or as if she'd just shut it.

'Goodbye, Blanche. See you later.'

'You're rushing off so quickly . . .'

'I'm late, Blanche, goodbye.'

'Goodbye, Louis.'

Louis stepped out on to the drive, between the hedges. What a filthy old drive it was, all mud and water. There'd been a storm in the night, and he hopped from right to left in an effort to avoid the puddles. Why on earth do we live in a place like this, he thought, when we could have a ground-floor flat in the centre of town. It was Blanche who wanted this rotten little house. Which meant that he had a twenty-minute walk to get to the solicitor's office where he worked, and he always arrived with muddy shoes. When you work at a solicitor's you like to have clean shoes – and a clean shirt. That's only natural, isn't it? Well, isn't it? And I had asked for a clean shirt, after all.

Mud and puddles everywhere. It's best to stick really close to the hedge, like this. Louis was munching on a small leaf that he'd plucked from the hedge – but then he worried that he might have a speck of green between his teeth when he arrived at the solicitor's office. He spat it out and passed his tongue over his teeth. It's such a shame, he thought, about Blanche: she's gentle, she's quiet, and she's quite pretty, so why is it that she's so – well yes, I'll say it – so stupid?

Damn it, I forgot to . . . Louis looked left and right: there was nobody about, so he could safely go up against the hedge. Barely worth it! A little shake of the legs and everything was back in place. Yes, Blanche was stupid. When someone spoke to her all she could do in reply was smile, because she was so kind. In short, Louis thought to himself, I, Louis, deserved better than that. I do love her; well, I sort of love her; but she's a stupid woman.

Louis hopped and skipped his way down the road, missing the puddles. He shrank into the distance, getting smaller and smaller until distance overtook him and obliterated everything.

Blanche, in the kitchen, was still standing in front of the cupboard with her hand on the door, as if she had either just shut it or was about to open it. She could open it, or else she could go on waiting. She had to wait, but for how long? She had to wait until peace was resumed.

She'd been near the table when Louis's words had reached her through the layers of the air around her. But instead of cutting cleanly and resonantly through the air like an arrow, the words had had a disturbing effect. Everything should have been so straightforward: 'Blanche, is my shirt ready?' 'Coming, Louis, coming.' She could have taken the shirt upstairs, helped Louis to attach the cuffs, and come down again, peace in her heart and all around her. She'd been near the table, and the shirt was in front of her, neatly ironed and folded, all starched and shiny.

As she passed her hands round the collar, there had appeared beneath her searching fingers a tiny thread caught in the starch, marring the shine that she had thought was immaculate. It was then that Louis's words had reached her – not cutting through the layers of air but disturbing them. Blanche had not answered;

she'd gone on smoothing the collar so as to make the thread disappear. 'Blanche!' he'd cried, in tones that now disrupted and cut through the layers. Still Blanche had not replied; she smoothed the collar faster, completely taken up with her task. She opened the cupboard and slipped the shirt in, waiting, her hand still on the closed door, for Louis to call out to her again. And, ultimately, for everything to revert to a state of peace. Peace – my God.

It was then that Louis had passed the kitchen door with his hat and coat – 'Goodbye, Blanche'. She waited for the layers of air to re-form themselves and be healed, for them to join up again and for the air to be one, without fissure or tremor, and for peace to inhabit her. She opened the cupboard and looked at the white shirt, folded and shining, on the ironing-board cover in the corner. 'Blanche, is my shirt ready?' She could have taken it upstairs to him . . . if only she could recreate that ill-conceived moment, give it a perfect birth. But you can't wipe things out and start over again just like that. In the stifling air, Blanche could only wait.

On the stove, a pan of water began to boil furiously, in huge bubbles, spitting noisy little drops on to the metal surface. 'Oh, for heaven's sake,' said Blanche, 'give me a minute.'

Again she looked at the shirt, and then shut the cupboard door. She stayed in the same position, her hand resting on the door, as if ready to open it one more time. But the pan of water went on issuing its calls for help.

'All right, I'm coming,' Blanche said.

She picked up the pan, emptied it into a washing-up bowl, filled it again, put it back on the stove and started to wash the dishes. But when emptying the pan into the bowl some water had run down the outside and it immediately began to hiss again. The hissing went on, and every other moment a drop of water spat on to the stove. It was as if the pan had a hole in its pocket.

'You're getting on my nerves,' Blanche said.

At last the fire managed to consume the water and the noise died down. In the silence that followed Blanche could feel all the suffering that was in the air around her. She grabbed hold of the full pan with both hands, plunged it into the washing-up bowl and put it back on the stove. 'You were right,' she said. 'Just carry on as before.'

Then Blanche dried the plates. In no time at all she had run the tea-towel first over the hollow part, then over the base and finally over the edges. Loyally, she used precisely the same movements for every single plate, no more and no less for the one that was a little chipped, and which she slipped into the middle of the pile: no need to expose its unhappiness publicly. Though after all, she thought, whether perfect or cracked, one plate ends up much like another – in little pieces in the waste bin. It's all grist to the mill, the final windmill of the plates: it's just a stage, that's all. The final windmill. The finishing point.

No, she thought, I mustn't think like that while I'm just at the end of drying this saucepan. My thoughts are saturated with that idea, and as all the gestures I make are saturated with my thoughts, the saucepan, back on its shelf, will retain the imprint of my gestures . . . it would sit there, infused with all the unhappiness of the world, and it would spread it all around itself, like a fluid.

Although the saucepan was dry, Blanche began to wipe it again, forcing herself to use movements that seemed natural, indifferent. Again and again she ran the tea-towel over the enamelled edge of the pan. The final windmill. No, carry on wiping . . . To the finishing point. No, wipe, wipe, wipe . . . It seemed as though a sea-swell was surging up inside her, an immensity of fluid stretching out everywhere. A wave of visions came to her, one on top of the other: snatches of conversation, muted reproaches, the image of a child – a child's body lying in a man's arms. 'Madame, the child was playing in the field, on the way back he was knocked over by a lorry!' 'Madame, the dog has bitten the child, the dog has bitten the child's throat!' Do you remember that man lying on a lorry, his mouth open, his mangled bicycle next to him? News items from all over the world, each one locking into another like pieces of chainmail, recalled by each movement of Blanche's hands on the ever more glistening saucepan.

Suddenly, in mid-movement, holding the pan close to her body, Blanche stopped, rooted to the spot. If only this dangerous minute could stop too, this minute which might enter into the shaping of destiny, exactly as it was now . . . Fortunately only

Blanche had been present when she had given birth to it and only Blanche had the power to revive it. If only the moment could be wiped out, once and for all . . .

The saucepan was clean and polished but the remains of the stew which it had contained were still sitting there on a plate. Blanche tipped the stew into the pan and put it on a corner of the stove, just as it had been at the time when the minute had started. There was nothing for it but to wait, to start all over again. She ran her hand over her forehead and the rest of her face. Oh my God, please give me one moment of peace . . .

She opened the door into the garden. Nothing to do but wait . . . and yet so many necessities remained to be dealt with before Louis and the child came home. So as not to waste time, she decided to go out and dig up some leeks for the soup. She loosened them with a spade and then pulled them out by hand, one by one. She was calmer now, because she was kneeling on the ground and because the clods of earth surrounding the leeks fell off easily when she shook them. A transparent red worm, only half visible, struggled to free itself from the earth. She might have killed it with the spade, Blanche thought; she only just missed dispatching the creature to the earthworms' final windmill. Laughing, she broke up the earth around the worm and watched it wriggling about in the hollow of her earthy hand, well and truly alive.

She threw the leeks in a pile on the edge of the path. After breaking up the biggest clods of earth with her hands on the patch of earth she had just disturbed, she smoothed it all over with her palms and stood up straight. She picked up the vegetables and walked to the kitchen. Her bunch of leeks in her arms, Blanche lingered for a moment on the threshold.

In front of her, beyond the hedge, there was a meadow, and then a road; and beyond the meadow and the road there was a big corn-field. The sheaves of corn stood tall and straight as if rooted by their own strength, stretching upwards in the heat of the sun. The sky above was incorruptible, all-powerful. Blanche looked, first once and then again, at the corn-field and at the sun. Her eyes were wide open, she didn't try to shield them as she watched the glistening corn beneath the summer sky. Her face burning, she could see the field and the sky joining together, the sun sending down the full force of its rays, twisted in sparkling coils or trailing down, the sun itself slipping as it whirled down towards the corn. It was a chaos of yellow fire, a miracle of heat and twisting shapes that was going to spread all over the earth – not to devastate the world but to embrace it and to merge it with the fiery sky, so that earth and sky and the whole universe became one. My God, Blanche said, my God, are you there? Is it you, this force, and are you nothing else? Or are you elsewhere, further away, beyond this force, so that it depends on your will? Or is it only my burning eyes? Oh God, where is your sign?

Blanche's eyes lost some of their fire as they focused on a nearby meadow, where a cow was ambling to and fro. It looked a strong, peaceful animal and she felt the desire to walk towards it and fondle it. She'd walk into the meadow, pat its horns and say, 'Poor old cow, so strong and peaceful, and yet so alone . . .' Her view of the world now crystal clear again, Blanche began to howl with laughter, because she could well imagine herself saying that to the cow, and what would anyone think if they saw her? She went on laughing until she remembered – pull yourself together, Blanche – that she had some washing to do. She turned round and, stepping into the kitchen, was on the point of collecting the bowl. But then she thought: before doing that, perhaps it would be better to . . .

She looked at the saucepan on the corner of the stove and poured the stew out on to a plate, just like she'd done the first time. Then she washed the pan again, this time gently, her face at peace. Slowly she dried it, with very careful movements, and put it back, spotless, on the shelf next to the other pots and pans. Looking at it again, she said, 'You're all right now. Keep to yourself those blobs which my still fiery eyes inflict on you: green, yellow or red, shut them inside you, enclose them in your enamel. Keep them to yourself and let them radiate from you in a beneficent halo . . .'

('Hello, Mama, I've brought you my school report . . . and I'm so hungry. Quick, give me some bread and jam . . .')

Blanche carried the wash-bowl outside on to the wooden trivet and began the washing. She was in a hurry; before this evening, she had to rinse and blue the linen, lay it out to dry, peel the vegetables and make some soup. She'd better stoke up the fire: not with a pair of bellows like some people did, but with her own breath. Kneeling, she blew into the stove every breath of air in her lungs. Let the fire exist through me, she thought, and let me exist through the fire. My life is made up of a thousand necessities, or a thousand complicities with water, with enamel, with soap, air and fire. And that is exactly how it should be, for they are necessities that must be accomplished if a household is to remain clean, and if Louis and the child are to find their food ready for them.

All the time she was doing the washing Blanche could see herself: she could see Blanche washing and, even though she didn't move away from the trivet, Blanche breathing into the fire, Blanche washing the stew-pan, Blanche contemplating the sun, Blanche making the stove shine. This is my place, she thought, between fire, water, iron, earth and wood . . . Here I am completely myself, I am Blanche, and it is here that my task lies. Failing to accomplish this work would mean risking isolation from the universe. This is me, Blanche, these are my legs, my head and my arms.

As if to grasp a better understanding of herself, she raised her arms and drew herself back a little. She stood there, her wild black head framed by her raised arms still slightly dripping with soapy water, her chest straining beneath the pink linen apron. This is me, Blanche, and I shall never know who I am. She lowered her arms, plunged her hands back into the lukewarm water and stood stock still, head lowered, hands immobile, watching the foam as it died, with a light sound, around her wrists. This is Blanche . . .

Louis and the child came home to find the kitchen tidy and the table laid, and when they had finished their evening meal Blanche washed and put away the dishes. Louis read the paper, which was spread out over the table, while the child cut out a picture. Blanche sat next to them darning a woollen sock.

'Blanche,' Louis said, 'Is there any beer?'

She got up and poured him a glass.

'Blanche,' Louis said, 'you haven't forgotten to iron my shirt?'

'It's ready,' Blanche said. 'It's in the cupboard.'

He leaned over the paper again; Blanche returned to the sock.

'Blanche . . .' Louis said.

She didn't like hearing her name spoken on its own like that. Nor did she like the colour; she never wore white dresses, and she preferred red roses to white ones, black hair to blond. She didn't like snow, because it covered the colours of the earth and concealed the life beneath.

'Blanche . . .' Louis said.

Why does he call to me with that dead name?

Blanche looked around her – at the stove, the sink, the cupboard and the pile of linen which she'd had to leave half-dry when a summer storm had suddenly darkened the sky. Then she looked at Louis and the child. All these objects and the man and the child, they made up such a strange sight . . . Yet surely there was nothing sad or tormenting in a man reading a paper and a child cutting out a picture?

Blanche looked again. Could it be that she didn't love this man and this child? No, she did love them – she loved them so much that she would throw herself into an abyss or into flames for their sakes. And that was precisely where the tragedy lay. Otherwise she could simply look at them, faintly moved, imagining that she was lightly stroking their hair – 'There's a good boy, there's a good child.' One at either end of a kitchen table: a man reading a paper and a child cutting out a picture . . .

'Blanche . . .' Louis said.

Perhaps she should have soaked and resoaked that shirt and then have boiled and boiled it again . . . Or perhaps it was the darkened sky, or her own name – which ought to be totally scraped away and obliterated so that she could be called Jeanne, or Marguerite; or perhaps it was her own heart, which ought to be smashed, smashed to smithereens . . .

There would be nothing to be gained from shouting out, nor even from weeping softly, and there was no point in looking at the pan, which refused to divulge its blobs of light. There was nothing for it but to wait for time to pass, to let it wash over her, and over the man reading the paper and the child cutting out a picture. Would nothing, no colour, no smell, come to deliver her? Quite soon Louis would say, 'Blanche, it's time for bed.' And she would feel that little knot of distress in her chest, she wouldn't be able to look calmly at any of the objects, and she wouldn't receive any co-operation from them either. All through the night she'd lie there in the darkness with her eyes open, her heart full of wild searchings. Would nothing come to her, no sign at all? The sock was in her hands and through the hole she could see the sewing-egg that she'd slipped into it: it looked like a white window. No sign, no sign. And soon Louis will say . . . Suddenly she put the sock down on the table and said:

'I forgot to collect the milk. Will you come with me, Jean-Louis?'

'Oh yes, Mama.'

'At this hour?' Louis said.

'The farmer's not in bed yet,' Blanche said. 'We'll need some milk for breakfast.'

She wrapped the child in a coat with a pointed hood, threw a shawl over her shoulders and they went out together.

'Don't take the child with you,' said Louis. 'It might still be raining.'

'It isn't cold,' said Blanche.

Louis drained his glass and put it down on the table, shrugging his shoulders. This was the latest: she'd forgotten to collect the milk. And while on that subject, he thought, I'll get my shirt and take it up to the bedroom. He went to the cupboard and took it out. He was just about to close the door when to his astonishment he noticed a bowl full of boiled milk.

'Forgetting to collect the milk is one thing – but forgetting that she *had* collected it, that's too stupid for words.'

Blanche hurried along the path, holding her child by the hand. Some drops of rain were still falling but the heat of the day lingered and the air was warm.

'Shall we walk through the wood?' Blanche said.

'It's all black in there, I'd be frightened,' said Jean-Louis.

'You mustn't be afraid of a wood. We might see some squirrels in there . . .'

'Squirrels? All right then,' said Jean-Louis.

In the wood the ground was soft and wet. Holding the child's hot hand tightly in hers, Blanche strode calmly into a dark, dank universe, its silence interrupted only by their light footsteps and by drops of rain on the leaves. She sat down on the bare wet earth at the foot of a tree and pulled the child on to her knee, wrapping his coat more tightly around him.

'Rest there,' Blanche said, 'and close your eyes. If you do that the squirrels will come out and put nuts in your pockets.'

'Mama . . .' said Jean-Louis.

She held the child close. Close to the earth, the trees and the clouds, she felt good. And inside the dark mass of coat on her lap there was the whitish blob of a child's face. As she leaned over him she could smell the sweet smell given off by the damp woollen coat and, when she stroked the forehead and hair of the whitish blob inside it, she inhaled the smell of her little son.

The child began to snore softly. Blanche leaned back against the bark of the tree and looked up at the sky. Yes, she felt good. A sense of peace rose up softly inside her, the peace of a universe that was wet with the wood and the sky. Not that it was a happy or easy peace – nothing was happy or easy, either inside or outside her; it was a fiery peace, a peace that meant all is well; the truth may be concealed but it is straightforward and powerful, like the trees and the sky; life is woven on a background of forces that are both straightforward and obscure, like the wet earth, like the sky, like the tenderness of the flesh, like love. In my life, Blanche thought, there are trees and sky, there is water, earth and air, there is the child and there is Louis. My life is beautiful.

She leaned over the child and listened to his breathing, then moved her legs a little further apart so that he had more space to snuggle into. Some clouds separated themselves from the moon, lighting up Blanche's wild head and the sleeping infant. She could see water glistening on the leaves, and then it was dark again.

Will there ever be love in my life? she wondered. Now love, that would be . . . She closed her eyes. Just suppose, for example, that a man came up to me in the wood: a young, strong man, wearing a velvet or leather jacket and trousers kept in place by a wide belt of material slung low on his hips. Why would he be dressed like that? Because that is how I see him: and because it is an attractive costume. He'd pass in front of me and we'd both look very serious. He'd say: 'Put your child down,' and I'd lay the child on the ground, and he would cover him with his jacket, saying, 'The children of women can never be cold.'

He would take me on the leaves of the wood, in the silence of the night. There would be silence between us and our embrace would take us to the heart of the trees, the water, the sky and the air, and the corn beneath the sky. It would be as if we were touching the knot of life itself; as if, while we were making love, we were at the very heart of the universe. And afterwards he wouldn't say anything – that he loved me or found me pretty – he'd just disentangle the leaves from my hair. He'd say nothing of his life, nor I of mine. He'd say, 'Off you go now. You are my wife, for all my life and all yours, perhaps even longer than that. If we should ever happen to be passing through the wood on the same day, we'll come together again, and love each other. There's no better gift we could give each other, for there's nothing greater in the whole world than to have been together, for one moment, at the heart of the universe.' He would leave, and I'd either see him again or I wouldn't. And there would be love in my life.

The wood was deeply peaceful. Blanche could sense the tree standing behind her like a pillar of life, and the child in her lap was as hot as a nest. The layers of air were unbroken, without the slightest scar, finely soldered on to the infinity of the night. She could go home.

Louis would say, 'It's time for bed,' and she'd answer, 'Yes, Louis,' and take a long, understanding look at the table, the stove, the coal in the bucket, the haloed saucepan.

The child stirred in her lap, mumbling a word from his dream. Blanche thought he said 'water' but perhaps she hadn't heard it right, perhaps he'd simply said 'aaah', an expression of admiration or pain.

'What are you dreaming about?' she said softly. 'Are you happy, are you sad? Answer me, Jean-Louis . . .'

Dreams help me, Blanche thought. The child didn't wake. She got up, still carrying him in her arms, and made her way across the wet earth, between the tall trees.

René

René

René crossed the little shop, lifted the torn curtain and stopped by the white enamel basin that was occupied by a woman's upside-down head. He poured out some soapy liquid and rubbed it in, then repeated the process, first washing and then gently massaging with both hands. As usual he could feel the slippery soap under his fingers, but today there was something else: today his fingers were discovering another, subtler softness, the softness of hair that was unusually fine.

Time passed. He gazed out of the window at the landscape, its wide expanse of sand, its pebbles and stubbly tufts of grass. As he continued to caress the unaccustomed softness beneath his fingers, René's mind went a complete blank. Time passed and still he hadn't finished.

'How long it's taking,' the voice said.

'Oh, I'm sorry, it's finished now,' said René.

He glanced at the upside-down head but the eyes were shut, the face closed. He rinsed the hair, moved the basin away and dabbed gently with a towel. Now he was touching a cascade of damp, light, sleek curls, which he smoothed out, combed, and then smoothed out again. Absent-mindedly he asked:

'What shall I use for friction?'

He listed names and makes but she didn't respond, so, following the advice of the manager, he gave her the usual sales talk.

As if to settle the matter once and for all, the voice said:

'I'd like some pure lavender.'

Nobody ever asked for lavender. René went to a cupboard and found an untouched bottle, with a hand-written label.

'We've only got it in bulk,' he said.

'That's all right,' she said.

He poured out the liquid, but all he could smell was the spirit.

'I'll call the manager,' he said, 'so that he can do your set.'

'No, don't do that,' she said, 'I just want it dried as it is.'

To dry it as it was, that was unheard of. You couldn't use the automatic drier because if the hair wasn't raised on top of the head in curlers the heat wouldn't reach it all, so he'd have to use the hand-drier, as he did for little girls. What's more, it would take at least half an hour. He picked up the hand-drier.

He ran the hot air over the head – or rather, he held the drier still for a moment at every stage, so that he could see each lock become lighter and lighter as it fell back into its natural waves and floated gently of its own accord. And all the while the scent – of the lavender now, not the spirit – became stronger and stronger, until it took possession of him, entered every part of him. He stood there, steel drier in hand, and because the noise was quite similar to (though in other ways quite different from) the noise at the munitions factory where he worked during the week, he could also see himself standing in front of his machine, as he passed his lathe over the steel casting and smelled the lubricating oil in the air all around him. Through the smell of the oil every detail stayed clear in his mind: he knew that he had to lower the lever with the red handle and that the procedure should take three minutes; he knew that in half an hour, work would be over and he'd go for a snack with his mates.

René felt as though he were inside a cloud in which there was nothing but the smell of lavender and this cascade of extra-ordinarily fine, vaporous hair that he was holding up in his left hand. It was floating now, fluttering like a ringed, golden bird under the hot air. He touched it, he raised it, he ruffled it gently with his fingers; he spread it out in a fan shape on her shoulders; he lifted its entire mass up towards the light, so that the cascade became clear and alive. From its waves the triumphant scent arose, and he could see, as if they had come to life that very moment on the cascade, the fine stalks and blue flowers of the lavender: at first just a few, and then an infinity of them, a swelling mass of blue. Vast, borderless lavender fields – though whether they were actually in front of his eyes or elsewhere, in some distant unknown place, he couldn't be sure.

'How long it's taking . . .'

Yes, next to the hair there was a face. He could see it in the mirror. The eyes were open now, and very close to him as he bent forward, but they weren't looking at anything visible in front of them, neither the mirror itself nor the objects that were reflected in it. Only the iris of the eye stared into the glass: pale blue with a touch of mauve. The eyes were lavender blue.

René felt apart from the world: he was inside a cloud filled with the smell of lavender, borderless lavender fields, and eyes that were lavender blue. And the more the cloud offered him, the greedier he became. What did it matter that she had spoken? He stayed where he was, his movements arrested as he held the drier over the fluttering hair. She too remained still, her eyes far away.

René looked at her face: it was impassive, even-featured. The local sun had given it some colour and the skin was pink and brown. He could not see her shoulders and her figure because they were concealed by the little white protective cape, but he could see her full, knee-length, blue linen skirt and her bare legs, smooth, brown and very beautiful. Why on earth had she come here, a woman like this? There was nothing in this forgotten village apart from one dismal hotel. What was she doing at the village hairdresser, which catered only for local girls wanting to doll themselves up for Sunday?

This impassive woman with her far-away eyes, asking for pure lavender and telling him, in her slow and unsullied voice, how to dry her hair . . . Why couldn't she say the things that everyone else said: that the weather was fine or lousy, that the sea was calm or choppy, that she wanted her hair to be crimped, and to look nice and glossy?

She was a peculiar, dangerous woman. René began to feel a preposterous rage, like a drunk's, rising within him. From inside his cloud he performed a spontaneous gesture that was as preposterous as his rage: suddenly, in a spirit of tenderness and a desire for vengeance, he bent over the impassive face and kissed it. He straightened up, blushing in shame and fear. Was he crazy or something? She was going to be furious, she'd cry out, and the cloud would burst; everything would become grotesque.

She didn't move. He could see her face in the mirror and it

revealed neither anger nor pleasure; he could see her inward-looking, blue-mauve eyes. Again he saw vast expanses of blue quivering beneath a gentle breeze. He leaned close to her hair, held it against his cheek, and kissed her face again. Then he looked right into her lavender blue eyes and said, 'Kiss me back . . .'

It was as if she hadn't heard him. He kissed her again and she put her hands on his shoulders as if it was a perfectly natural, simple thing to do. Tenderly and intimately René smoothed her hair, played with it, pushed it back behind her ears. She let him do whatever he wanted – and yet, my God, she still didn't smile. He said:

'Could you come to the stone path that leads to the sea, this evening, about six?'

'Yes,' she said.

He stood up, gently combed her hair, and gave it a neat parting down the middle.

'Is it all right like that?' he said.

'That's very good,' she said.

As he helped her unknot the cape he could see the whole of her blue linen dress. She picked up her bag and prepared to leave.

'Are you really going to come? Because you mustn't say you're going to come if you don't mean it.'

Pushing the torn old curtain along the rail, he called the manager. She went up to the counter and left the shop.

'Whew, what a stink,' said the manager. 'What on earth did you use on her?'

'Lavender,' Rene said.

The manager saw the opened bottle on the wash-basin and said, 'For crying out loud, that's pure extract . . . some chap sold me that once . . . you're only supposed to use a drop or two and dilute it with something else.'

'Oh,' René said.

'You ought to have charged extra for it,' the manager said.

'I'll make up the difference,' René said.

'Off you go, time for you to get on with the next customer,' the manager said.

The next customer was a little boy with long, straight hair.

He walked slowly: the air was heavy, and it was better not to hurry because it wasn't six o'clock yet. He was feeling good now, because he'd got rid of his white overall and was wearing his pullover and white duck trousers. He saw his friend Luco sitting on the ground mending his nets.

'How're you doing, Luco?' he said.

'I'm getting ready, it's going to be a fine night. Where are you off to?'

'Dunno . . . I'll be around.'

He went on his way and arrived at the stone path. Would it be better to wait like this, standing up, or should he sit down? He decided to go right to the end of the path and back, and then do it again, as if he was just out for a walk. He had only walked a few steps when he saw her sitting on the sand by the side of the path.

'I really thought you wouldn't come,' he said.

'Why?' she said.

He didn't know what to reply. She was sitting down and he was standing next to her.

'Shall we walk for a bit?' he said.

When they had walked a few steps he pointed to the end of the path, where piles of overturned, shattered rocks stretched ahead.

'Look,' he said. 'There used to be a flat jetty there, stretching all the way to the sea. But then it was mined, and it exploded. Shall we climb up the rocks? It's fun.'

He leapt effortlessly from one stone to another, sticking to one side and holding out a hand to help her. He was hoping that a false step might throw her against him, but she managed perfectly well on her own. At the very end of the demolished jetty they sat down on a wide, low stone wall. That is where they were and that is what they were doing at that precise moment. Still she neither spoke nor smiled. René asked himself what he was doing here, how he had dared to ask her to come. He also reflected that today might have passed like any other day – but because she was there at his side, even though he felt ill at ease, he was surrounded by something that was both confusing and extraordinary.

She spoke. 'Have you been a hairdresser long? Do you like the job?'

'It's not my job,' he said. 'I'm really a turner.'

'Here?'

'No, at the munitions factory. I take the bus every day. My dad put me into hairdressing when I was a kid, so I come and help Claude out when there is no work at the factory. But it's not my real job. Oh no – I'm a turner.'

'That's a lot better,' she said, 'because . . .' – she finished the sentence in a peal of uncontrollable, childish laughter – 'because hairdressing's a stupid job for a man.'

'Sure. You're making fun of me – but, after all, you go to the hairdressser, don't you?'

'That's because I've only a little wash-basin in my room here, and there's no hot water. Normally I wash my hair myself.'

'So when you and I go to the hairdresser, it's by accident, for both of us . . .'

He laughed, pleased with his little analogy, and she'd spoken at last, just like everyone else. He went on laughing – then abruptly stopped. She wasn't laughing, nor was she talking any longer. He began to feel uncomfortable again. But it gradually eased, without him even noticing it. She had leaned back and was half-lying on the broken rocks. He leaned back himself, so that he was right up close to her; he could smell her hair. He stayed like that, his eyes looking up at the sky, doing nothing, and he didn't feel bored. It was the first time, he thought, that I've stayed like this, doing nothing, the first time that I've looked at the air for that length of time. And the colour of the sky began to quiver in front of his eyes; the whole sky was covered with sea-swells and with lavender, as far as he could see, and beyond.

Then, because it was the only way that he knew of to appease his soul, he turned towards the silent woman. She didn't try to free herself; but she didn't help him, either. And being the man he was, there was no brutality or impatience in his actions; he was slow, gentle. She let him do what he wanted but she was immobile, frozen.

He felt all his strength and virility drain from him; he felt shame and anger at the same time. He shook her by the shoulders, crying out, 'Why don't you move, why won't you say something, do something . . .' Her body against his felt like a tepid corpse.

He felt quite alone with his shame and his anguish. He couldn't even insult her to get his own back, he couldn't say that she was one of those women who lead men on and then refuse to give themselves, since after all it was he who had invited her to come here, and since she had let him have his way . . . Was it his fault, then? But why hadn't she helped him? Oh, the bitch, the dirty bitch . . .

He started to pummel her. Under his harsh, violent blows, it was again as if she was letting him do just what he wanted. She didn't try to free herself by hitting back, she didn't cry out, she didn't complain. He hit her on the legs, on the arms, on the shoulders, but her limbs stayed firm, her flesh supple and taut. She parried the blows only with a kind of tension, an elasticity that scorned the brutality. Her only defence was her perfection.

'Why don't you speak, why don't you cry out? . . .' He stayed immobile for a moment, looking at her big wide-open eyes that made him think of a blue lake without banks, a sky without limits. He covered them up by turning her face to the ground, scratching it against the stones and the jagged concrete. He was consumed with anger in every inch of his being, in his hands as they crushed, clawed, tormented. Let her be crushed, let her be smothered – blue virgin, black virgin, unsullied virgin, let her stay there and die, let the tide carry her away.

He fled, jumping across the demolished jetty from one rock to another, running as far away as he could. He felt hot and he was still in the grip of a desperate rage. That such a shameful thing could happen to him, he who was always so successful with the girls!

After a bit he calmed down and walked more slowly. After all, he thought, what did she say to you, what did she do to you? Are you going to leave that silent, gentle girl, with her miraculous hair, lying there wounded on those rocks? He turned on his heel. Of course, he would help her to get up, he'd soak her handkerchief in the water, he'd gently wash her face.

Walking back along the stone path, well before he came to the jetty, he could see her a few steps away from him, sitting on the remains of a little demolished jetty. A bit of railing was still attached to the low wall and she was leaning against it, her arms wide apart, her hands holding on to two uprights. He could see her profile as she looked out at the water: her beautiful hair was in perfect order and there were no scratches on her face.

'I didn't hurt you, then?' he said.

'Oh, no,' she said.

'Even so, I acted like a brute. But what did you think you were up to, coming here to meet me like that . . . how did you expect me to behave?'

'I expect nothing, nothing . . .' she said, in her slow, gentle voice.

She was standing now, her arms still wide apart. Her image showed up clearly against the background of sea and sky, between the two uprights of the railing. She was only a few steps away from him, and yet she was so far. There was nothing for it but to leave her.

'You OK, Luco?'

'Fine. How about you, where've you been?'

'Nowhere.'

He walked slowly along the quay, towards the bottom of the village, where he lived. Mariette had prepared a tomato salad and a big plate of grilled sardines. She went up to him.

'Whew, how your hands smell!'

'Don't speak to me about smells. Leave me alone . . .'

'But it's not like the usual smell, it's sharper, let me think, what is it . . . Whew, what a stink!'

'Shut up,' he said. 'You're not to say that word. Just shut up, you hear me?'

'You're touchy today . . .'

Laughing, Mariette went into the kitchen and came back with the bread. They sat down to eat.

'It's Saturday,' she said, 'and the cinema's open. Shall we go there later?'

'Maybe,' he said.

She pushed the plates away and thumbed through a magazine that was lying on the table. René sat still, doing nothing, though every now and again he shut his eyes.

'This pattern for a summer skirt, I could easily make it up myself, with that printed fabric I've got. It's not difficult: fold it so, cut it so, and you're there. But it's not worth starting now, because we're going to the pictures. He doesn't look as if he's getting ready to go, though. Is he asleep? Still, he's less tired than when he's been at the factory all day. The programme begins at half-past eight, but we could go in after the news. I'll leave the washing up, I can do it tomorrow morning with the breakfast things.'

René closed his eyes. It's Saturday: she wants to go to the cinema. Saturday. His mind stopped, he couldn't think any more. All he could see were images. He saw her slim and tanned, her fair hair spread out. He saw unknown regions where endless, quivering fields were transformed into lakes without banks, and then into a sky of the same dazzling cruel shade. Was it real, or was it an illusion? He still felt intoxicated by the all-consuming blue glow of her presence and by the gentleness – smooth as glass, fringed with hoarfrost – of the perfection that was her magic defence against the world. He'd had to go, he'd had to leave her, but the memory of her standing against that beautiful bit of old wall, on the silent strand of a plaintive world, would always be with him.

'So, are we going to the cinema, or aren't we? Is he sleeping or not? If I shake him he'll be livid, but if we hang about any longer we won't be able to get in. And I'm bored . . . I would have done better to start cutting out that skirt. Are we going or not? It'll be too late to go soon. And I'm so bored, doing nothing like this. You shouldn't have to do nothing on a Saturday.'

And from now on, René thought, it would ever be thus. Because of her, because of the memory of her – or rather because of the borderless fields – he would never again be bored doing nothing. He didn't know whether or not the images sprang from her; it wasn't really important. The important thing was that from now on they would always be there. Every time he stood up in front of his machine, his lathe, they would be there, either within him or outside him. He would shave the casting with his lathe and the steel turnings would spin off, smooth and bluish, and he, René, would have no importance at all. Even his movements would be slightly more important than him.

Less unreal than he was, the images would become his whole life. He didn't know where they were but he felt strongly, now, that they were outside him, beyond him. They had either come to him of their own accord, or from her, the source of images. They would be there whenever he was doing nothing or when he was standing in front of his lathe. They would always be there, stretching palely out before him, eloquent as only silence can be. They would attach themselves to his life like an obscurely related story. From now on, all festivities would be sad occasions, false diversions in his life. At the fringes of the night, his images would be the sole harbingers of dawn, as if bringing hope in their train. René felt that he was carrying a burden heavier than despair.

'We won't get in to the cinema now,' she said. 'Are we going to play cards or are we going to stay like this?'

'Let's stay like this,' he said.

Sous le pont Mirabeau

Sous le pont Mirabeau coule la Seine
Vienne la nuit sonne l'heure
Les jours s'en vont je demeure.

GUILLAUME APOLLINAIRE

Illustrations by Mig Quinet

Sous le pont Mirabeau

Lying on her back in the bed, she stretched gently. Now that the pain had gone, a feeling of great happiness suffused her whole body – a childish kind of happiness, the sense of well-being that follows pain. From head to toe – in her flesh, her heart and her mind – she'd reverted to a state of total childishness, and if any words came to her at all, they'd be those of some silly song. 'One-eyed snail, lend me your feelers, one, two three . . .' Was that how it went, or had she got the words wrong? What peace I feel, she thought, inside me and round about me . . .

She turned her head to look at the tiny face beneath the netting. And smiled. Well, she's certainly not beautiful at the moment, still hot from her mother's waters and blood – a vague, shadowy little creature. So far there was something missing in her: it was as if she hadn't yet been liberated, touched with grace; tomorrow she would be beautiful. Tomorrow the dawn would have touched her face, her nostrils would have inhaled scents and smells, her body would have been bathed in air and the intervening hours would have dried her hair, smoothed her hands. By tomorrow she would have taken her place in the universe, she would have settled firmly among the beautiful phenomena of the world. She would have become a phenomenon herself.

Tomorrow, as soon as dawn comes, as soon as she feels the sun, she will be beautiful, this little newborn child of May. Oh the beautiful month of May . . . blind snail, lend me your feelers, I've stopped feeling pain, and I'm going to sleep now, really sleep . . . Peace inside me, and all around me.

A loud noise broke her sleep. In her half-conscious state, she thought it must already be dawn; a man must be standing on top of a lorry chucking an empty dustbin on to the pavement. Two dustbins, ten dustbins, a hundred dustbins. Leaning on her elbow she turned towards the shaded window, but could see nothing. Sleepiness and childishness rolled off her; the pain she had recently felt and the well-being that came after it became states of the past. Restored to normality, she could distinguish every sound clearly. Now she knew exactly what she was hearing: rosaries of bombs and gun-fire that mingled with each other and got louder and louder until they turned into a cacophany, sustained by the rhythmic breathing of the sirens.

She sat bolt upright in the bed, without thinking about whether her body would say yes or no, leaned across to the child, picked her up and drew her close. She no longer heard the sounds from outside; they shrank into the background, infernal but unchanging. The sound of windows rattling and walls shaking seemed to be so close, and to come at such regular intervals, that it no longer surprised her. It was the inside noises that she was listening out for now: footsteps, running steps in the corridor, bells ringing again and again, the sound of voices. She was waiting for heaven knows what to happen.

A nurse came in, panic-stricken:

'You're not supposed to move! You mustn't be frightened, it can't be an attack because we're not at war, are we, not in our country. It's just the anti-aircraft guns, there are a lot of planes passing over, and they're firing at them . . .

'And you're not supposed to touch the baby, you know! A rule's just been made that they must be left in their cots . . .'

The worried nurse picked up the baby, dumped her back in the cot and went off, crossly.

She hadn't responded or protested to the nurse but as soon as she was alone she leaned over again, took the baby in her arms and held her very close.

She could pick out the sound of an engine coming closer, as if a plane was diving, swooping back up and then diving down again. Twice the whole building trembled, from basement to rooftop, in the space of a few seconds. She looked at the window near the bed, at the window-panes. Hail, Mary, she thought, Hail Mary full of grace . . . Mary might have been full of grace but she wasn't timorous. One fine night she stopped somewhere, got down from her donkey to give birth and then got straight back on the donkey to continue her journey. If only she could just get to the corner of the room, so that she could stand up with the baby next to the cupboard, far enough from the windows . . .

She threw off the blankets and held the baby close, tucked in her left arm. With her free hand she groped around, looking for something to support her, then, sliding out of the bed, she tested her legs. Her head span, her legs buckled, and her body gave way under her. She lay down on the bed again and closed her eyes for a moment. Ah well, she thought, the Virgin Mary was the Virgin Mary, after all; I am only me. I'm going to need two or three more hours' rest – then I'll be able to move, I'm sure of it. The windows and the walls have stood up to the bombardment so far, and no doubt will continue to do so for two or three more hours. Leaning back against the pillows she stayed there, quite calm and still, clasping her baby in her arms.

How quiet the room had been on that first day, filled with sun, the sunshine warming the blankets and her hands that lay motionless on top of the folded-back sheet. But the wave of silence was strangely unreal; it was an anguished silence because of the contrast with what was happening elsewhere. She propped herself up a little and turned towards the window, straining to catch the words and sounds wafting up on the air, trying to imagine what was happening in the street.

'I can see something shining up there . . . I bet they're going to fire.'

'I think I can see something too – a long way off, between two trees?'

'There are lots of French soldiers on the ramparts . . .'

'Oh well, that's all right then.'

But the nursing-home was in a side-street, a long way from the centre, and she couldn't often hear anything very significant; mostly she just heard the same noises again and again. They seemed to respond to each other and to repeat each other so monotonously that they were tedious, irritating – they seemed pointless. After the alarm siren would come the gunfire, and she'd count the muffled, rhythmic shots – loud, soft, distant, close – then there'd be silence again, and the 'alarm over' siren would sound. Minor hubbubs that no longer bore any resemblance to the chaos of the night, minor hubbubs that marked the passage of time and frayed the silence.

The cup and the plate that she'd used for lunch hadn't been cleared from the table and the nurses were up to their eyes. Trolleys were rushing up and down corridors; doors were opening and shutting and telephones ringing; it was as though the night's tumult had preciptated a wave of births, a constant flow of women in labour. It seemed as if every baby that was supposed to have been born in the fortnight to come had decided to be born on that day.

Looking around her, she saw the cup and the plate, the suitcase she'd left on the chair when she came in yesterday morning, the flowers in the vase, the enamel-painted table and bed. She felt the strength of the sun on the blankets, on her hands, and on her face, and she felt the peace and silence of the room – this room of hers that had been abandoned by time.

She straightened up a little and took the child in her arms. The air was heavy with smells: the smell of the lilies-of-the valley in the vase, the smell of the wooden furniture, the smell of the different fabrics in the room. Now the air had brushed the baby's nostrils, the sun had touched her hair, and time had smoothed her hands. In the dawn hours her mother's hands had touched her cheeks, her mother's warmth had impregnated her body. My beautiful little daughter, here is your first day on earth.

The road had come to life again.

'Seems things aren't going well at the border . . .'

'It'll take some time before reinforcements arrive . . .'

Closing her eyes, she could see roads, villages, stations, frontiers. New images came to her, grafted on to other images from the distant past; they intermingled, alternated, became jumbled up in her mind. Memories came to her from the source of her being, from the beginning of time. And through the sounds, words and smells of today, past times came overwhelmingly to life, in all their minute details.

She recalled a morning in August, as stunning as this morning in May, when she'd been an innocent child holding her parents by the hand, a child who, not knowing the meaning of possessions, without memories of her own, was leaving nothing behind her. She had seen the river Meuse downstream, never upstream before. From new roads, new towns and unfamiliar country, she learned, for the first time, the meaning of discovery. She watched hands joining and parting, handkerchiefs waving, and she learned the meaning of friendship and the agony of parting. On a station platform she saw a woman kiss a man, kiss him again and drench him in tears. As she watched the woman turn away, stumble against a pile of leather equipment, haversacks and mess-tins, and lean desolately against a wall, arms empty and heart wide open, she learned the meaning of conjugal love. And when the train stopped in the middle of a field, as the sun was setting, bathing everything in beauty and turning the trees purple and gold, she learned something of the sweetness of an evening landscape.

As she lay in this furnished room she heard, from the depths of her being, the voices of her mother's father bringing her home from school, telling her that one day at Isaphan a gardener had been afraid of death. She didn't really understand, but it was good to feel his rough hands in hers, and to learn the meaning of memories. Her schoolbooks might be able to tell her that her country was divided into nine provinces, that the world contained five continents, that John heard Jeremy's dog barking, and that René ate rice and made fun of Robert – but now she was learning from sentences like this: 'Snacks available 24 hours'; 'Saponite washes whiter'; 'When you hear gunfire keep to the right-hand pavement'; 'On to the bridge-head'. Legs aching, eyes wide open, she walked on through the wide jostling avenue, full of fumes from the brightly lit stalls. She was at the very heart of life.

This May morning had become mixed up with that August morning long ago; here she was at the source of her memories, at the very source of her being. The stillness in the room and the noises outside made her susceptible to the plight of that child from the past; it was as if the child was calling out to her, and she felt a lump in her throat.

She felt sure that the very colours and sounds, the very sensations through which life revealed itself to her, inhabited the same streets, people, trees, rivers, fragrances and daylight as they had for that child from the past, still so alive in her memory. From you to me, she thought, from me to that other child; perhaps, today, just from you to her . . .

In the meantime, the fortifications erected by the men were falling to soldiers who were as handsome as they were strong.

2

There were people everywhere, men, women and children, twenty or twenty-five in a lorry, seven or eight in a vehicle meant for four. She was stretched out in the back of a lorry, her tiny baby on top of her, looking straight ahead with impatience in her eyes. She'd brought it upon herself, she thought, getting caught up in this escape – yet she wasn't really fleeing or abandoning anything, she was merely responding to an appeal. The clarity of her memories guided her like a star.

She didn't dare look around her yet; she was allowing her body time to adjust to the bumpy ride. Touching her strangely slack belly she readjusted her dressings, made sure her milk was coming through and checked that the baby was properly covered up. Then she closed her eyes for a moment, trying to distract herself, to think about something other than the wheels bumping over the road. She was frightened, in spite of herself.

The first few hours passed quickly; she knew the road well, and anyway had no control over the passing of time. Then, reaching a queue of other vehicles, the lorry slowed down and a queue began to form behind it. So long was the convoy that you couldn't see either the end of it if you looked back or the start if you looked ahead. It seemed as though the whole human race was on the road: men and women, young and old, ugly and beautiful, in cars, lorries, bicycles, tricycles, push-chairs, hand-carts – even on foot, carrying heaven knows what possessions in their arms.

Engines over-heated and the vehicles came to a halt, defeated by the slow pace. The border was at least five kilometres away. On the right-hand side of the road there was a large building set among green trees and terraces where you could sample all the products that came from bee-keeping. First five, then a hundred, then a thousand starving people rushed to this place and came out with their arms full of paper bags: honey sweets, honey gingerbread, honey caramels. Lord, what a lot of honey in this dawn of war.

But where is the war? And who is the war? Perhaps it would be easier if one could find a symbol for it. But the memory of a great helmeted goddess, strong, impassive, feared, revered and dispensing glory, for whom soldiers would enlist and lay down their lives, had faded now. Perhaps she was all around us, behind and in front and among us, crumbling and above our heads . . . perhaps that was her symbol overhead, see, three fine bombers passing through the sky of an early summer. People looked up, gingerbread in hand. 'Take cover, for God's sake, take cover!'

But it was hard to know where to take cover; the road was now full to bursting. The bombers passed over without firing. How good the honey was, slipping so meltingly down the throat.

Shouts of departure, and everyone dashed to the lorries before the doors clanged shut and they got going. They travelled at least two kilometres at top speed, which seemed a hopeful sign, but then the convoy stopped, blocked by another going the other way: this one was made up of big waggons covered with tarpaulins stretched over hoops; soldiers led the horses that pulled them. This convoy stopped too, brought to a standstill by the traffic jam, and conversations took place between the two.

'Where are you supposed to be joining up?'

'We're going to Ostend. We're supposed to await orders there.'

'Cigarette?'

'I won't say no . . . like some wine?'

'God, I'm dying for some.'

'Your people must be hot, packed in like sardines in this sun.'

She raised herself slightly, holding on to the handle of one of the doors with her right hand, supporting the baby with her other arm, and looked at the soldiers. She was less interested in their helmets and jackets than in their faces, and their eyes, and the colour of their hair. The two that were talking were tall and thin, Parisians called Jacques and René, and there was another one, the youngest, who was stout and blue-eyed and determined-looking. He'd unbuttoned his jacket, he was suffering badly from the heat. Their faces, eyes and whole bearing were those of grown men, but if they were asked their names, they'd give them in full, including all their first names.

'Looks as though the road's clearing . . .'

They raised their hands in salute and exchanged good-luck farewells. Still half propped up, looking through the mica panel in the hood of the lorry, she watched them go. Some of them remounted the horses, others set off on foot alongside the trucks, others sat at the back of the lorries. The whole convoy moved off. No shots were aimed at the sky. All those feet on the road, soldier after soldier, taking long masculine strides, each with their own way of walking, their own special characteristics.

'God Almighty, I'm hot. D'you want a cigarette? They're Belgian, it's good tobacco. "If you've a Lucifer to light your fag . . ." '

'Idiot. Shall we eat some of that gingerbread that the kid gave us? Hey there, horse-rider, would you like a piece of ginger-bread? While we're going so slowly you might just as well stretch your legs.'

All those feet treading the dust with long masculine strides. Lucien-Georges Gaudinet, Pierre-François-Emile Forgeron, Albert-Amédée Léridan. No shots had been fired at the sky. She could still see the soldiers, in the far distance, but only just. Farewell, unknown soldiers who weren't leaving for war.

She lay down again in the well of the lorry. And now this convoy got going too – not surprisingly, since they had each blocked the other.

She looked at the baby: she could start to drink her mother's milk now. She half-opened the big dressing-gown that en-veloped her completely, and tried to unbutton her nightdress, but it was too tight.

'Has anyone got a pair of scissors?'

'Yes, but they're at the bottom of a suitcase that's at the bottom of the lorry . . .'

The material finally gave beneath her fingers and teeth, releasing her swollen breasts.

It's not easy to put an infant to your breast for the first time. The baby tried to suck, gave up, tried again, then gave up altogether. She held her head against her, sensitive to the slightest movement from her baby's clumsy lips. She was vaguely aware of some commotion around her but, preoccupied with her task, she barely noticed that the lorry had stopped again. She moved in the anxious, rather awkward manner of the new mother. The baby drank a little of her milk, and she buttoned up her nightdress and sighed; she was exhausted. This time they had stopped for good: it seemed the border was closed, and no one else would be able to cross it today.

The activity on the road was at its height but on both sides the meadows and fields were quiet, drenched in heat. The great peace of the evening was rising slowly from the very edge of the horizon.

Some women emerged from the houses that were dotted along the road, with water, wine, blankets; one of them offered mother and child a room for the night. Seeing that there was something going on and that a woman was being helped down from a lorry, the soldiers who had stopped on the other side of the road came up to them and said, 'Hang on a minute, we'll help you out.'

They came back with a stretcher, and within moments they'd got her on to it and were carrying her. The house was tiny, the stairs winding and narrow. After several tries at mounting them one of the soldiers said:

'There's nothing else for it, if we're going to get round that corner we'll have to stand the stretcher upright.'

'We mustn't do that,' the other one said. 'I know what I'm talking about, if you stand up abruptly it can bring on an embolism.'

Laughing, she said:

'There's no room for an embolism in a place like this! Come on, help me stand up.'

Then she quickly added:

'But take the child, because if I were to fall . . .'

The third soldier, who was leading the way, leaned over and took the baby, holding her almost at arm's length, as men do.

Once the corner was turned, they lowered the stretcher and went into the room. It was very small, with a bed so high that it almost touched the low ceiling. One of the soldiers took the woman in his arms, and as he carried her to the bed he stumbled, so that they both nearly fell; all four of them laughed. When her baby was given back to her she held her close, sighing with relief.

'Thank you,' she said. 'And I can't even offer you a drink . . .'

They chatted for a few moments, and the soldiers told her that the traffic jams on the road had separated them from their regiment. There were quite a few of them, in two lorries, and they didn't know whether they were meant to join the others in

Ostend or in Furnes. One of them had gone off to make a phone call; he would be back by now, they said, so they had better go down and find out.

How odd, she thought to herself: a very small room, simple, clean and bare; a woman, a newborn child, and three soldiers.

It was a bold and beautiful morning, like yesterday and the day before, and through the little window in the room she could see wide, peaceful fields. Above them the light was vaporous and you could smell the nearness of the sea: the green, grey North Sea.

She took a few steps around the room; she seemed to be all right. After all, she couldn't always have a stretcher and three soldiers to help her.

Her companions from the lorry helped her downstairs but when they got outside she walked on her own. She sat on the bench in the lorry, like everyone else: that made an extra place and was something of a relief to those in the front, who were sitting on top of each other. The lorry started up, she felt the wheels turning and turning. An hour, an hour and a half, two hours . . . and then suddenly it speeded up, until they were going very fast, and they crossed the border almost without noticing.

'Carry on, carry straight on. No, don't bother to show your papers. Go on, and hurry.'

When they came to crossroads, there were sometimes police or soldiers signalling them on. It was like a fever of haste. And everyone did what they could, went as fast as possible, even tried to overtake, but there was no point, because you only had to dovetail back into the convoy.

Arriving at dark Dunkirk, they crossed the town at speed. They saw some sailors sitting around on walls – waiting for something, perhaps, or just bored. After that the convoy spaced out, cleared a little, some vehicles taking one direction, others another. Now it was possible to overtake, as some vehicles went more quickly than others. Four or five lorries went past, one behind the other.

The baby was making some progress with feeding and had drunk all the milk from her mother's breast, but she still seemed hungry.

They stopped for the night in a village in the Somme. It was always the same: lorries banked up at the side of the road or in courtyards, and houses full, so the last arrivals had to sleep in the vehicles or in barns. A woman came out of one farm and, seeing the mother and child, said:

'There's still my bedroom, come in quickly now and make yourself at home.'

It was no good protesting that she could walk: as she got down from the lorry, a soldier took her in his arms and carried her up to the house.

She sat down in a wicker armchair near the stove, her baby asleep in her arms, a brown and white cat rubbing up against her legs. The kitchen was full of soldiers. When she came in they'd been eating their meat and beans but now they were more interested in the woman and child, staring at them, forks in the air. One of them said, pointing to the baby: 'Well, there's someone who's not worried.'

They went back to their food and from time to time they looked at her again, smiling gently at her, perhaps because she seemed so tired, to cheer her up. The farmer's wife came back and said:

'The room is ready. But there's no electricity, so you'd better change the baby down here.'

'Yes,' she said, 'And it's time to feed her, she's beginning to fret.'

She told the farmer's wife how the baby cried after a feed, and that she still seemed to be hungry.

'It's because you don't have enough milk,' the woman replied. 'It's a real problem. I've had eight children, and I went through it with the last two: I had to give them three bottles a day.'

'That's all we need!' she said, in a flat voice.

'Let's have a look.'

The woman went up to her and pressed her breast: she managed to produce a few drops of milk. The men stopped eating again: they were quite still, waiting to see what would happen. Silence weighed on the room. Finally the woman said:

'It's not marvellous . . . not to mention the fact that your milk probably isn't very nourishing. They're fatal, those long journeys by road, they make you so tired.'

'I've a bottle of condensed milk with me, I'll give her some after I've fed her.'

One of the soldiers opened the tin with his knife. Some milk spilled over his fingers so he licked them.

'Look at Armand, he's guzzling the mother's milk,' somebody said, and everyone burst out laughing. She asked the soldiers how long they were going to stay in the village.

'We've been here several days already. Tomorrow at dawn we're going to Dunkirk, and there we await our orders.'

'Dunkirk?' she said. 'We've just come from there . . .'

'And we're just about to go there . . .'

Another said: 'And while we're waiting, we're all here together . . .'

The soldiers, the young woman and the farmer's wife all looked at each other and smiled.

Washed and changed, the baby slept contentedly in her mother's arms. She was sitting in the wicker armchair again, resting her head on the back of it. She was waiting, because the woman was making coffee for the soldiers and had told her that she ought to have some too, because it would do her good. The lamp was very dim and shed a great golden halo on the table, over the hunks of half-eaten bread and the quarter-full bottles of wine; the rest of the room was bathed in a half-light, the soldiers settled where they could. One had taken off his jacket, rolled it into a cushion and stretched out on a bench near the wall, his shirt half-open; the brown and white cat curled up in a ball on top of him, its paw on his smooth young chest. No one spoke. All you could hear was the noise of the coffee-grinder as the woman slowly turned the handle, and the baby sucking her lips in her sleep.

When the woman had finished grinding the coffee the smell filled the entire room, and the atmosphere became even more intimate. The soldier lying on the bench, stifling in sweetness, let out a deep sigh, and said in a child's voice:

'How good this place makes you feel.'

The farmer's wife said, 'I wish you could stay on here.'

Silence took over again until a distant voice emerged, as if from the shadows:

'I heard someone say just now that they've occupied Brussels.'

'I was there yesterday morning,' she said.

3

She hoisted herself up on to the enormous bed. She'd installed the child next to her on two chairs pushed together, and she let her hand hang over the side of the bed so as to be able to touch her – she seemed so far away down there. Exhausted, she went to sleep straight away.

At dawn she was woken by the footsteps of the soldiers leaving. She could hear them shouting at each other:

'Come on Robert, we're waiting for you! Why are you taking so long?'

'I can't find my notebook!'

'What notebook?'

'A little address book with a red cover. Maybe it's in the barn, I'll go and look.'

After a few minutes someone shouted out:

'Well, have you found it?'

'Hell, no . . .'

'We'll come and help you.'

Footsteps on the paving-stones in the courtyard faded in the direction of the barn. Then they came back and passed beneath her window again. The sound of their footsteps altered as they reached the road, and soon she could no longer hear them.

She didn't get back to sleep. As daylight began to filter into the room she could make out several rosaries with large, carved beads hanging on the wall, and a highly polished mahogany bed, with starched sheets and pillow-cases, initialled in red cross-stitch. Suddenly a ray of sunlight lit up the room, so she could see clearly the face of the little girl sleeping down there on her two chairs. She was getting more and more beautiful.

The vehicles set off again. But she looked out of the window and saw, just for a moment, the open door of the big kitchen and the cat warming itself in the sun.

The sun was really strong, the countryside beautiful. Sometimes they had to stop so that she could heat up a little mineral water on an alcohol stove by the side of the road to add to the condensed milk, for she had less and less of her own milk.

How sombre, how sad, Boulogne – encircled by huge balloons, captive, heavy in the sky. Soldiers everywhere – in the

streets, in the houses. In Boulogne you had to go into banks and
bureaux de change to have the money in your possession inscribed
on your identity card, and while these formalities were under-
way, she waited for hours with her baby in a small café. The
room was full of English soldiers, and she watched them closely:
their uniforms were finer than those of the French soldiers and it
seemed as if they were less embarrassed by them, that they
suffered less from the heat despite the heavy material, the kit-
bags, the guns. They seemed, too, to have managed to forget
their names.

She walked up and down the room, trying to send the baby to
sleep. At the window, she pressed her face up against the glass.
The streets were full of people who were strangely silent, and the
big balloons looked fixed in the sky; she felt heaviness and
oppression in the air. Turning away she went on walking up and
down. The soldiers weren't talking, they were lined up on the
café benches as if they were storing sleep, gathering their
strength. She felt very alone, caught up in the great apparatus of
war. She tried to find a single face on which to rest her gaze. The
baby raised one arm and uttered a little cry; she quietened her
by leaning against her face. They stayed like this, their faces
buried in each other's.

Under her large dressing-gown, she could feel a trickle of
blood running down her leg. She hadn't had a chance to attend
to herself for several hours now. She could see a door marked
'lavatory' on the far side of the room but to get to it she'd have to
disturb this great pack of silent soldiers. So instead she sat down
at a table and slowly rubbed one leg against the other to wipe
away the trace of maternal blood.

In the evening, the beach at Crotoy was golden yellow, purple in
places. In the morning it was a brilliant white, already too hot,
and everyone wanted to bathe, to stretch out on the burning
sand, to find instant solace from the anguish and uncertainty
around them; they wanted to stay here, to wait, and to revive.

She heard a commotion on the road. With a noise that was a
cross between clanking and spluttering, a strange car came into
view, its windows broken, its bodywork smashed, its wings
ripped off. It slowed and stalled, with an odd sound. A man
emerged and said:

'I've been shot at. My car turned over three times, over and over. The engine's still going, and so am I . . .' He laughed, thinking himself touched by the grace of God.

They drove along beautiful roads lined with trees, roads that hadn't been surfaced nor always well repaired: roads of earth and stone, roads that you wanted to walk on, that made you want to sing.

The road was white-hot, with banks covered in willow-herb and grey signs that came and went: Abbeville 10, Abbeville 15, Abbeville 20. The four vehicles met up with the main road via a smaller one, seven kilomètres south of Abbeville, and they all travelled at high speed, the noises of the engines intermingling. Suddenly a man ran out into the road. Wearing a blue peasant's smock and a straw hat, he was gesticulating at them with his stick.

'You want to take cover,' he said. 'They've sounded the alarm in the village, there's going to be action right above us.'

The vehicles stopped and everyone got out.

'Come this way, to the crossroad, under the trees.'

She leaned against a tree trunk and bent over her baby: the peasant stood leaning against another tree opposite her, his hand on his stick.

The time had come, and in the sky above them the planes moved away, came together, swooped down on each other, while gunfire crackled from right to left, above and below the road. Then there was an explosion, a loud bang, and the man said, in his country accent:

'The bloody idiots, they're dropping them anyway, their filthy bombs . . .'

He counted them, banging his stick on the road as he did so.

'There they go again, bloody idiots, they're unloading near our village, in the heart of our fields . . .'

Suddenly he was off, making his way towards the village where the bombs were falling. He strode away, his stick raised, brandishing his fists, powerful in his rage.

Silence returned, and so did the beautiful hot road, all earth and stones. Abbeville 25, Abbeville 30. Abbeville was further and further away, and as soon as the dull murmur from the town hit the road, it seemed to fade into nothing. Was it time to feed the child? A few minutes to go yet . . . She was piecing together the scraps of a sentence in her mind: Abbeville . . . Abbeville, in the Somme . . . what was it? All of a sudden the sentence came back to her, in its rectangle of words, the sentence that she'd read a hundred times over:

'Published on the . . . by F. Paillart, at Abbeville (Somme).'

At Gravigny, where they had to stop for the night, all her travelling companions found rooms. In a kind of kitchen-dining-room, a local schoolteacher served mutton chops to her and to his daughters, Jeanne and Valentine. They were sixteen and eighteen; they had sad eyes and moved softly. He went out and came back with some bottles which he placed on the table. He said:

'You can drink this without worrying: it's only home-made wine. I made it myself, with apples and rhubarb.'

He raised the blind a fraction and looked outside:

'They're still arriving . . . There won't be room for them all tonight, where are they all going to sleep?'

He sighed and poured out more rhubarb wine. On the armchairs and floor were coloured silk cushions embroidered by Jeanne and Valentine.

Gravigny was a small seaside town, pinkish grey, with turreted houses and white railings; there were many hotels and garages. In the evening the roads were dark yet they thronged with people, bumping into each other, interrupting and questioning each other, still hoping to find somewhere to spend the night. It was full of people and quite dark, until the great green and red arc lights shone out over rooftops, walls and faces.

She stayed still for a moment, the child in her arms, overawed. Above her was the beauty of the guns. A second of immobility was enough to embrace, and reject, the beauty of the guns, denuded, useless, miraculous, valuable only in their own right. But what if this beauty was meant to become embedded in the secret of all things, to flourish in the greens and reds of nature and the rhythms of the earth? Or perhaps to be exploited, warped, faded, false as the beauty of the helmeted warrior and his steel blade, false as the beauty of the dead hero – kissed, corrupted, rejected? Above her was the beauty of the guns.

People took refuge in shelters, standing close to each other, elbows touching, shoulder to shoulder. For how many hours did she hold her child above people's heads so as to save her from being smothered? It seemed like an omen.

Evreux 5 . . . Evreux 10 . . . Evreux 15 . . .

4

The cathedral of Chartres stood intact, miraculous, majestic, blending with the sky.

A little further down the lorry stopped near a bend, and everyone got out to have a drink. But instead of going into the café with the others she lagged behind, leaning against the wall near the windows. She felt that if she took another step she would lose all her blood. Looking through the window into the café she saw a room, blue with smoke and full of soldiers. Outside, the street climbed up to the square and opened out to show the cathedral bathed in sun. The houses were quiet and peaceful, still preoccupied with the business of everyday life. She could hear young, passionate voices rising and mounting to a crescendo: the soldiers were singing. Blood still trickled from her body, staining her legs, sometimes flowing for minutes on end. The sun warmed her hands, burned her forehead and her face, and the child was rather heavy in her arms.

Her body was suffused with warmth and tenderness, as from a slow, sweet exhaustion. She thought of the man she loved, of the way his fair hair fell over his eyes. One of the soldiers sang a line from an old song and, because they all knew it and liked the irony of it, the others joined in: 'That's a lot better than catching "scarlet fever".' Their voices were strong and happy, but the moment the joke began to pall, they became slow and monotonous, as if they were only singing to stave off boredom.

A train heading for Paris started up and whistled at the nearby station. Two soldiers passed and she heard one say, 'How the time drags . . .' Then two others: 'I'm famished.' 'Here, have a piece of chocolate . . .'

She looked round at the quiet, simple houses, at the sun, at the searing beauty of the cathedral, at the tiny baby in her arms, and she felt love in her heart – for the singing soldiers, for the blood flowing down her legs, for the soldier munching chocolate, for the sweet brown earth of the Beauce. Her throat swelled, and joy and happiness rose up in her: her memories were intact, they were present and all around her, and her heart, alive and warm, was in harmony with them. All around she perceived the world's splendour, its pain and its joy: in the sweetness of the air, in the sound of the men's voices, in the colour of the earth, in the halo created by the stones, in the simplicity of a movement, in everyday remarks, in the tenderness of a look, in colours, sounds, the light of the sun.

She raised her eyes and looked again: 'Oh God, protect your church, let every one of its stones be saved, and let none of these singing soldiers die.'

The Sologne was a lush, green place; its villages had sonorous names, like Fort Saint-Aubin, and the sky above the woods and the marshes was peaceful. When a villager offered her a room, she spent a whole day resting, letting the vehicles and lorries go by. In the evening her hostess watched over the baby while she went out. She walked along with tiny little steps. There were no lights but the sky was clear; the roads were deserted and cars were parked along the pavements. She passed two soldiers sitting outside a shop-window, and one of them said:

'Where are you off to, all alone?'

'Well, I'm looking for a . . .'

'Why don't you look for it later – come and sit here with us.'

Hearing youth and boredom in their voices, she went and sat between them; they all linked arms, and one of them leaned towards her, resting his head gently on her shoulder as if in a kind of trance. They were silent for a few moments until one of them said:

'What was it you said you were looking for?'

'I was looking for a café. I was hoping there might be something left to eat.'

'You're not from the village either, then?'

'No, I'm not.'

'Come on, let's go and look for somewhere together.'

They took her along with them but she couldn't keep up with their pace.

'What's wrong, do your feet ache?'

'No, it's not that . . .'

She went on, speaking very quietly:

'I've just had a baby, she was born on the 9th of May.'

They said, 'Oh . . .' In the darkness she couldn't see their faces very clearly, but she could sense that they were confused, a bit thrown by what she had said. They took her by the arm again, walking at her speed now.

When they found the café it was packed, with villagers as well as people passing through, all gathered round a wireless set. The same speech was being broadcast for the third time, with that sentence about a miracle. They sat down at a table but the owner told them there was nothing left to eat.

'Nothing at all, not even bread and sausage?'

'Nothing. We haven't even eaten ourselves, I was serving non-stop till nine o'clock. There'll be more again in the morning.'

'OK, shall we have a drink?'

One of the soldiers nudged the other and said, 'Look, André, see that bottle of decent brandy, that'll warm us up.'

'You're not cold are you, in this weather?'

'Not really . . . that's to say, I am and I'm not.'

'*Patron*, three brandies, if you please!'

André got up and went over to the wall. 'Look, a map of France . . . It's one of those that show where all the different cheeses come from – funny.'

'Hilarious.'

Back at the table, they clinked glasses and downed their brandy in a single gulp.

Outside there were the deserted streets, the stationary vehicles, and the sky: fine, clear and starry, making her feel a little sad. The soldiers linked arms with her and pressed their bodies lightly against hers. With tiny tiny steps they took her back to her lodgings.

In the Indre there's a beautiful village with a large central square and a smart hotel used by travellers en route for their holidays: it's called the Hôtel de la Promenade. When they arrived there were so many people on the terrace and so many in the village square that you'd have thought there was going to be a fête. To these people, an open lorry was like a cage of wild animals from a travelling circus, and inside the cage were lunatics, cared for on their journey by each village that they passed through. Today, their nurses were taking refreshment at the Hôtel de la Promenade.

She put her baby in a wicker basket that she'd bought on the journey: the baby seemed happier in it. With this cradle tucked under her arm, she knocked at the door of the solicitor's house, where she was to spend the night. There she was shown to a magnificent bedroom, with Empire bed, Empire wardrobe, Empire chairs, Empire cradle. Worn out, she sank down, dimly aware of an intoxicating smell that came from the ground floor: of meat cooked in wine, and a fruity sugary scent that made her think of the solicitor's wife standing in front of a vast red copper basin, making – what sort of jam? Too early, surely, it's only May . . . Calmness filled the whole house, and warm air drifted in through the open window. She saw red and blue lupins in bloom against the wall of the house, and heard birds singing in the trees. Then a voice broke the silence:

'Babinette, will you fetch me a bit of parsley from the garden? Quickly, darling . . .'

She heard a child's footsteps.

That night there was a lot of noise in the village. Just before dawn a company of soldiers had turned up, setting up camp in a lane opposite the central square. Were they or were they not going to cook up some food? Of course they were. Let's throw papers and wood into the roaring flames, let's make a good blaze that will throw up flames high, high into the sky . . .

Then a plane spotted the fire and peppered the whole area with incendiary bombs. A soldier said, 'That's not fair play, just as we were going to eat.'

Nothing fell on the solicitor's house.

By morning the square was peaceful again, for most of the vehicles had already taken off and the soldiers and their lorries had left the village.

The lorry she was in pulled out on to the main road from a side street and she could hear the whirring noise of a hundred or so bicycles making for the South: kids of fifteen to eighteen on their way to Toulouse. The lorry came to a halt, blocked by this great movement of young hearts, this surge of pure spirits, this vast wave of idealism. Ambivalent and irresolute, their faces were pale and dusty, streaked with sweat, which made them look older than they were, and their eyes were heavy with the need for sleep. They looked what they were: tired children who had just travelled hundreds of kilometres.

The lorry left the road again for a cross-country route that would be quicker than the overcrowded highway. The baby sometimes opened her eyes wide now, for several minutes on end. Her face was beginning to take shape, to live.

A warm, light breeze did not disturb the chestnut trees of the Corrèze but a tall poplar, an uneasy exile, stirred with a sound like distant water. The mornings were dazzling. By the afternoon the sun had risen above the bare-topped hills encircling the horizon, and the air was full of the scent of dry grass and heather. Evenings were still, and nights full, light and starry, the sky at peace: in this area, nights had become human again.

Dressed in a checked cotton overall she had bought at the village shop, she would walk round the grey and white houses, sometimes going down as far as the pool to watch the children fishing or chasing the eels that slithered among the reeds. She'd go back when the sun began to set but would linger in the chestnut wood, sitting on the grass and the dead leaves, held back by the sweetness of the air. She dreamed of a house somewhere on the road, with its own little cottage garden: in the evening, the man she loved would come home, take her in his arms and hold her close. Nights would be quite silent, like last night and the night before that, and they would be followed by days that held no fear. Fine, warm nights, nights to make love in ... Tears came to her eyes. The baby stirred in her arms, and she breathed in her faint breath and her milky smell, bending over her, finding a little comfort in her small daughter's warmth. Would they ever come back, those carefree days and nights?

Every evening at the inn the men gathered round the wireless set, drinking gentian-bitter, Pastis or sweet beer, and chatting about what they'd just heard; then, one by one, they'd go home. The days slipped by, sunny and peaceful, and every day the men would gather round the wireless set. The village began to lose its tranquillity as men and women from the road turned up and stayed on, while Belgian soldiers passed through in lorries, straggling soldiers on their way to somewhere or other.

There was fighting at Dunkirk.

A wind began to get up in the village, which made it difficult for the baby to breathe. Sheltering in the church porch she shifted the shawl on the tiny head. They could hear children's voices breaking into song after the catechism: 'Sacred heart of Jesus . . .' The voices rose, sharp, high-pitched, slightly off-key: 'Save, save France . . .' The words were preposterous, ridiculous, unbearable.

In Gardone they found themselves in a garden that reminded her of Italy. They had thought they were following the route but the road ended in this little garden full of palm trees and flowering laurels, wild and mysterious, with no owner in sight. Eventually an old woman with a Dordogne accent appeared on a path and directed them to the nearest inn. As the vehicle reversed, everything began to sparkle the way it does in Italy. Was it something to do with the place itself, she wondered, or was it the hour – that moment when the sun disappears in a mass of dying red rays? Or was it to do with the unusual brightness of a particular day?

The inn had a large, ancient kitchen where everyone ate, and inter-connecting bedrooms on the first floor. Hers was the room at the end. In a vast wooden bed the baby looked lost, like a little elf in a fairy-tale. A fierce summer storm wracked the night sky and when she got up to close the window she thought she could hear other noises between the thunder-claps: bombs falling or bursts of shellfire. Maybe they were blowing up munitions at the Bergerac explosives factory, or maybe some bombers had lost their way in the storm. She thought she could hear engines, muffled by the sound of the torrential rain, approaching, receding, returning; then a series of short, sharp explosions, distinct from the fuller, louder, echoing background of the thunderclaps. She lingered at the window before closing it. Bright flashes of lightning lit up the roofs and the garden, and night briefly recalled day as objects took on their usual colour and shape. Freshness and the sweet smell of ozone filled the air. Suddenly she thought: 'If my baby and I have to die in this war, please let it be from the sky's natural thunder.'

5

Lying beneath pine-trees on the edge of a wood in the Landes, in an old-fashioned pram belonging to a woman from the village, the little girl smiled for the very first time. The sun, peeping through a tear in the pram's hood, shone a star on to her cheek. It was that time of day when heat is beginning to ease, and smells drift up from the over-heated earth. On the other side of the road a thin dark-skinned boy, moving jerkily with a can on his back, was treating some vines with sulphate.

She heard the sound of a horn, distant at first, then getting closer; through the pine-trees at the bottom of the wood she could see the Beautiran-Cabanac train. It was time to go back. There were only eight or nine houses in the hamlet, and the men and women who lived there had come out to discuss the news that they had just heard on their wireless sets. The Germans had entered Paris. A woman standing in an open doorway was the only villager who seemed unmoved by the news. As if replying to a question, she said: 'What's the point of crying today rather than yesterday, or any other of the days we've lived through? Not that we had reason to cry on any of those days either . . .'

Her eyes shone bright, her face a picture of serenity. She made no effort to explain what she meant but said, looking at the little girl fidgetting about in her pram: 'You mustn't waste time: this child must eat every day that God sends.'

Every day, at the end of the afternoon, the mother took her baby for a walk. She'd follow the road up the hill past some vineyards and stop at the entrance to the woods. Or she might go down to the village, where there was the church, town hall, baker's, and a café. This took longer because the road was stony, and one of the wheels of the pram had lost its rubber tyre: it sounded like a cart. Military trucks were parked under the plane-trees in front of the town hall, and there were usually soldiers about, sitting on the running boards or on the steps of the church porch. They'd wander in and out of the café and play with a young blackbird that they'd tamed and adopted. When they got bored with doing nothing they'd play a peaceful game of cards, and the blackbird would jump from one shoulder to another. They didn't make jokes, and there was nothing cheeky about them:

they had serious faces and a thoughtful expression in their eyes. Sometimes you would see the faint glimmer of some secret wish deep in their hearts, something you had to sense without mentioning it or drawing attention to it. Were they perhaps guided by a higher force, something inexpressible that had been instilled into them, something that emanated from every living creature?

'Are you here for long?' she asked them.

'We're awaiting orders . . .'

She'd heard that phrase from so many of them now. She could remember them all: the men she'd met before they got to the border, who'd carried their names all over their faces; the men who'd carried her on a stretcher; the men at the farm, whom she'd heard leaving at dawn; the men she'd heard singing in Chartres. All these men had been awaiting orders. But there was one order which they already had, which no one had given them, but which was more compelling than those which might or might not yet come. It came from the very depths of time or perhaps from the edges of the future.

She went up to the soldiers, spoke to them again. Smiling, they showed her the blackbird and told her what it liked to eat. All the way back to the hamlet she thought about them and their buried secret.

The news came faster and faster, got worse and worse. People talked of the Loire as a rampart of steel – but water is only water, and Frenchmen are only men. The days got hotter and hotter, the grapes in the vineyards began to take shape. The villagers left their radios on all day and the news was interrupted by strange messages: one, two, three, four, five, six, and so on up to fifty or fifty-three. 'Twenty-five armoured cars approaching, abandon route 60, take route 80 . . .' On the road to the left of the hamlet, scent from the bullet-scarred pine-trees permeated the still air as the thin dark-skinned boy treated the vines with his jerky movements. The train from Beautiran went past: it was time to feed the child. 'Sixty-five armoured cars approaching on route 93 . . .' One, two, three, four, five, six, and on up to fifty-eight.

Now the wireless sets stayed on both day and night. The summer was relentless and the fields, which had turned gold, were all that shimmered in the faint breeze of the evening.

Today the fighting was over. How hot it was. Through the wide open window, the overwhelming scent of the pine-trees drifted in on the night air.

She went down to the village. The military trucks had gone and the square near the town-hall was empty. But other trucks had arrived in their place – huge, powerful, black – white deaths' heads painted on black bodywork. These soldiers were tall and strong, all young, mostly fair, with fine, well-cut uniforms. They didn't say much; calm and correct, they possessed the equanimity of a conquering army.

On her way back to the hamlet she stopped at the house of the inscrutable woman. They looked each other in the eye without saying a word. Because the pram had stopped moving, the baby had woken up. Then the woman said, 'You'd better keep on the move. And you ought to sing her a song, too.'

The woman went back into her house, put her coffee-pot to heat on the embers of the open fire, while the mother went on her way, pushing her baby's pram. Still, there was one memory in her heart that would never fade – of soldiers with serious faces playing a game of cards while a blackbird hopped from one shoulder to another.

All the past had to be lived again.

Life resumes its slow, difficult course: an odd, half-awake kind of life. The little girl learns to walk and talk. One day mother and child are standing close to each other, looking out of the window. The little girl sees a dog going past, and waves to a small boy; the mother is thinking of a huge band of earth stretching from the Meuse to Marseille. She hears people saying, 'France has been beaten by her army.' Smiling at her child, she points out a horse and cart in the street. The child is much too small to understand what her mother wants to say and besides, how can she possibly get it across? The thing is as ineffable, as nebulous, as the little girl herself; her senses and ideas have yet to develop properly. As the years pass she will become a woman, and have clear ideas about life.

'Listen, here's a nice song: Silly snail, lend me your feelers . . .'

But still the voices droned on:

'What's the point of scuttling the fleet, unless it's yet another sacrifice in the spirit of our defeat?

As for now, only a silence, and no danger of blasphemous thoughts.

Bibliographical Note

With the exception of the novella *Sous le pont Mirabeau*, which appears here for the first time since its original publication in French, the stories in *A Nail, A Rose* were published by Editions Tierce, Paris, in 1985, as *Sept Nouvelles*, in the Littérales collection edited by Françoise Collin. This was the first publication of 'Clara' and 'Champs de Lavande' ('René'), both written between 1980 and 1985. Publication details of the remaining stories are given chronologically, with the translated title, if different, in brackets.

Sous le pont Mirabeau: Editions Lumière, Brussels, 1944
'Les jours de la femme Louise' ('Louise'): *Les temps modernes*, Paris, 1947
'Un clou, une rose' ('A Nail, A Rose'): *La NEF*, Paris, 1949
'Anna': *La NEF*, Paris, 1949
'L'Aube est déjà grise' ('Leah'): *Empédocle*, Paris, 1950
'Blanche': *Voyelles*, 1981

Madeleine Bourdouxhe's other published work includes:

La Femme de Gilles (novel): Gallimard, Paris, 1937, reissued Editions Libris, Brussels, 1985
A la recherche de Marie (novel): Editions Libris, Brussels, 1943
'Les Temps Passés' (extract from unpublished novel): *Le Monde Nouveau*, Paris, 1956

Acknowledgements

Madeleine Bourdouxhe's work has barely been documented
and much of the information offered in this volume is the result
of new research in London, Brussels and Paris. I am especially
grateful to Françoise Collin, Marcelle Marini and Françoise
Pasquier for the help they gave me and to the Musée et Archive
de la Littérature for providing a photograph of the author.
Daphne Tagg in London and Doreen Vincent in Dieppe
provided invaluable editing and linguistic advice. I should also
like to thank Susan Bassnett, Scarlett Beaurain, Judith Chernaik,
Ros de Lanerolle, Suzanne Perkins and Lynne Stevenson. And
Dr John Stokes.

Faith Evans
February 1989